SCHOLASTIC

REALLIFE®

MATH

by
Eleanor Angeles

Note on Prices and Rates

All prices and rates quoted in this book are estimates by the author so that exercises can be completed with ease. Please check with your local transportation, telephone, financial, and other appropriate companies if you wish to work with actual costs.

●●●

We are grateful to the many students who helped us put this program together. Among those who deserve special thanks are Arnold Angeles (Carle Place High School), Siegfred de Guzman (Our Lady of Mercy School), Erik Galian, Richard Reyes, and Kenneth Perez (North Shore Public School).

The Real Life Math Staff:

Eleanor Angeles, Author
JoAnn Stevens, Math Consultant
Nancy Hoefig, Text Design
Whole Hog Studios, Text Illustrations
Ellen Taurins, Cover Design
Ron Morecraft, Cover Photograph

●●●

ISBN: 0-590-35476-0

Copyright © 1990, 1989, 1978 by Scholastic Inc. All rights reserved.
Published by Scholastic Inc.

26 25 24 23 22 21 20 19 18 17 16 15 14 13   0 1 2 3/0

Printed in tne U.S.A.

WHO NEEDS SCHOLASTIC REAL LIFE MATH?

Frank and Ernest   **by Bob Thaves**

NATIONAL BANK

HOW CAN I BALANCE MY ACCOUNT WHEN YOU KEEP BOUNCING MY CHECKS?!

To avoid Frank and Ernie's problems, read on . . .

You have been doing math for years.

Now **Scholastic Real Life Math** will give you experience in using math in everyday life.

To get and keep a job, you need math skills.
To run a home or a workshop, you need math skills.
In sport, travel, shopping—you'll use math every day.

In each **Unit** there are sections to help you learn and understand how to **use** your math skills.

Most lessons have a **Fact Box**. It is the information you might need to do the exercises.

You will be asked to calculate—to add, subtract, multiply and divide. If you need help to do this, go to the **Reference Section**. In the **Glossary**, you will find the meanings of words that you may need. Keep a working pad by you all the time. You will need it for calculations.

The **Looking Back** and **Skills Survey** pages at the end of each unit test your progress.

CONTENTS

Unit 1

UNIT 1

You are a mathematician. When you're buying groceries, counting change, or scoring a ballgame, you are using math skills. The exercises in this unit will help you to prepare for the real-life problems you will face later on in this book.

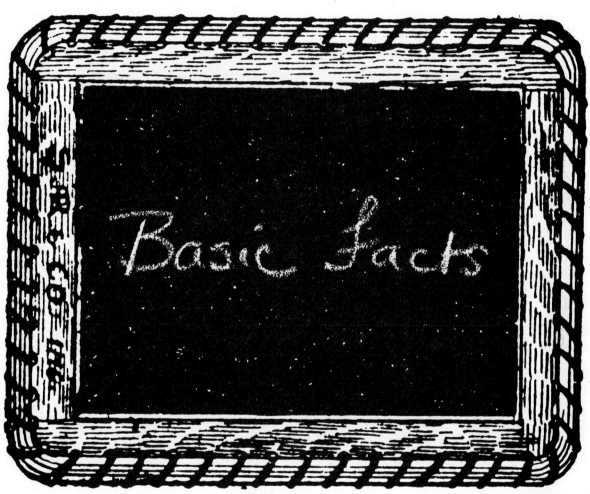

ADDITION OF WHOLE NUMBERS

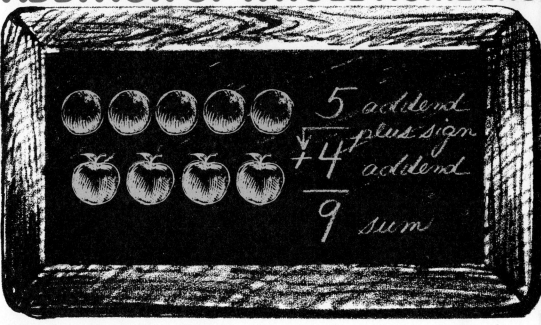

Which facts are missing? Put them where they belong.

ADDITION

+0	+1	+2	+3	+4	+5	+6	+7	+8	+9
0 +0 = 0	0 +1 = 1	0 +2 = 2		0 +4 = 4	0 +5 = 5		0 +7 = 7	0 +8 = 8	0 +9 = 9
1 +0 = 1	1 +1 = 2	1 +2 = 3	1 +3 = 4			1 +6 = 7	1 +7 = 8	1 +8 = 9	1 +9 = 10
2 +0 = 2			2 +3 = 5	2 +4 = 6	2 +5 = 7	2 +6 = 8	2 +7 = 9	2 +8 = 10	2 +9 = 11
	3 +1 = 4	3 +2 = 5		3 +4 = 7	3 +5 = 8	3 +6 = 9	3 +7 = 10	3 +8 = 11	3 +9 = 12
4 +0 = 4	4 +1 = 5	4 +2 = 6	4 +3 = 7	4 +4 = 8		4 +6 = 10		4 +8 = 12	
5 +0 = 5	5 +1 = 6		5 +3 = 8		5 +5 = 10		5 +7 = 12	5 +8 = 13	5 +9 = 14
6 +0 = 6		6 +2 = 8		6 +4 = 10	6 +5 = 11	6 +6 = 12	6 +7 = 13	6 +8 = 14	
	7 +1 = 8	7 +2 = 9	7 +3 = 10		7 +5 = 12	7 +6 = 13	7 +7 = 14		7 +9 = 16
8 +0 = 8		8 +2 = 10		8 +4 = 12	8 +5 = 13	8 +6 = 14		8 +8 = 16	8 +9 = 17
9 +0 = 9	9 +1 = 10		9 +3 = 12	9 +4 = 13	9 +5 = 14		9 +7 = 16	9 +8 = 17	9 +9 = 18

As you work on real-life problems later on in this book, you may forget a few addition facts. Use this bank to help you remember.

Adding from Right to Left

Add the ones.

1. **2.** **3.**

	301	a.	125	a.	617	a.	223
	452		243		321		132
	3						

Add the tens.

	301	b.	125	b.	617	b.	223
	452		243		321		132
	5						

Add the hundreds.

	301	c.	125	c.	617	c.	223
	452		243		321		132
	7						

Write the sums.

Hundreds	Tens	Ones
3	4	5
300	40	5

...*753*... d. .... d. .... d. ....

Using Your Memory

To find 5 + 3 + 9, you first think of 5 + 3 = 8, and then add 9 to get 17. Add two numbers first, remember the sum, and then add another number to the remembered sum, and so on.

Find the sums.

4. $2 + 1 + 5 =$ ....

5. $3 + 4 + 6 =$ ....

6. $4 + 5 + 2 + 1 =$ ....

7. $1 + 3 + 7 + 9 =$ ....

8. $6 + 5 + 8 + 7 =$ ....

Regrouping

How do you usually add 68 + 26?

$$\begin{array}{r} 68 \\ +26 \\ \hline \end{array}$$

A. Add the ones, 8 + 6 = 14; write 4. Remember 1 ten from 14. ☞ 4

B. Add the remembered 1 ten to the tens, 1 + 6 + 2 = 9; write 9 to the left of 4. ☞

$$\begin{array}{r} 68 \\ +26 \\ \hline 94 \end{array}$$

Find the sums.

9.

74	57	26	49	**12.**	126	782	365	485
+16	+38	+55	+48		+ 59	+156	+809	+760

10.

78	85	49	39	**13.**	924	864	346	984
+36	+75	+68	+84		+ 76	+247	+876	+249

11.

175	29	354	158	**14.**	1787	2528	2637
+28	+384	+296	+493		+ 907	+ 645	+7363

Lining Up Numbers to Add

Line up numbers by place value. Ones must line up with ones, tens must line up with tens, and so on. To add 23 + 1 + 3251 + 401, line them up this way:

```
  23
   1
3251
 401
```

Line up these addends:

1. 235 + 4 + 61 + 4000

2. 4312 + 34 + 5 + 789

Adding Long Columns

You can add long columns of addends in different ways. Study the following methods :

Method 1

```
 455
 658
 834
+212
```

```
  19  ← add the ones
 140  ← add the tens
2000  ← add the hundreds
2159  ← sum
```

Method 2

```
455 }
658 }  1113  (partial sum)

834 }
+212 } 1046  (partial sum)
       2159  (sum)
```

Method 3

Collect numbers that add up to ten.

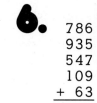

```
2 1 5 9
```

Find the sums using the method that's easiest for you.

3.
```
 124
 953
 687
+456
```

4.
```
 875
 235
 492
+618
```

5.
```
 267
 725
 128
+953
```

6.
```
 786
 935
 547
 109
+ 63
```

Checking Sums

One way to check your answer in addition is to change the order of the addends. You should get the same sum. Check your answers in Ex. 3-6.

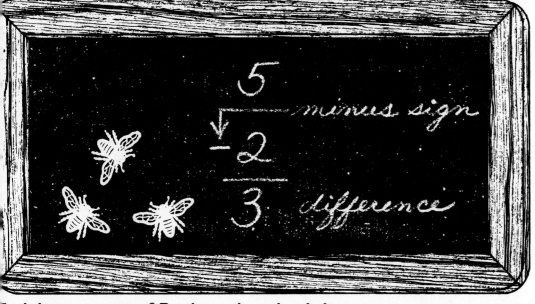

Which facts are missing? Put them where they belong.

0 −0 0	1 −0 1	2 −0 2		4 −0 4	5 −0 5	6 −0 6		8 −0 8	9 −0 9
1 −1 0	2 −1 1		4 −1 3	5 −1 4	6 −1 5		8 −1 7		10 −1 9
2 −2 0		4 −2 2	5 −2 3	6 −2 4		8 −2 6	9 −2 7	10 −2 8	
	4 −3 1	5 −3 2	6 −3 3	7 −3 4	8 −3 5		10 −3 7		12 −3 9
4 −4 0	5 −4 1	6 −4 2	7 −4 3		9 −4 5	10 −4 6		12 −4 8	13 −4 9
5 −5 0	6 −5 1		8 −5 3	9 −5 4		11 −5 6	12 −5 7	13 −5 8	14 −5 9
6 −6 0		8 −6 2		10 −6 4	11 −6 5		13 −6 7	14 −6 8	15 −6 9
	8 −7 1	9 −7 2	10 −7 3		12 −7 5	13 −7 6		15 −7 8	16 −7 9
8 −8 0		10 −8 2		12 −8 4	13 −8 5	14 −8 6	15 −8 7		17 −8 9
9 −9 0	10 −9 1		12 −9 3	13 −9 4	14 −9 5	15 −9 6	16 −9 7	17 −9 8	

SUBTRACTION

You may forget a few subtraction facts as you work on real-life math problems. Use this bank to help you remember.

Addition and Subtraction

Addition   Subtraction

$$\begin{array}{r} 2 \\ +3 \\ \hline 5 \end{array} \qquad \begin{array}{r} ? \\ +3 \\ \hline 5 \end{array} \qquad\qquad \begin{array}{r} 5 \\ -3 \\ \hline 2 \end{array}$$

Rewrite each item into a subtraction problem. Then find the difference.

1. $\begin{array}{r} ? \\ +9 \\ \hline 18 \end{array}$ **2.** $\begin{array}{r} 22 \\ +\ ? \\ \hline 28 \end{array}$ **3.** $\begin{array}{r} ? \\ +7 \\ \hline 39 \end{array}$

4. $\begin{array}{r} 35 \\ +\ ? \\ \hline 347 \end{array}$ **5.** $\begin{array}{r} ? \\ +213 \\ \hline 635 \end{array}$ **6.** $\begin{array}{r} 701 \\ +\ \ ? \\ \hline 705 \end{array}$

Renaming Numbers in Subtraction

How do you usually subtract 45 − 18?

A. Rename 45 as 3 tens and 15 ones.

B. Subtract, 15 − 8 = 7; write 7.

C. Subtract, 3 − 1 = 2, write 2.

$$\begin{array}{r} \overset{3}{\cancel{4}}\overset{15}{\cancel{5}} \\ -\ 18 \\ \hline 27 \end{array}$$

In each example below, the larger number is renamed before the smaller number is subtracted. Find the difference.

$$\begin{array}{r} \overset{2}{\cancel{3}}\overset{14}{\cancel{4}} \\ -6 \\ \hline 28 \end{array}$$ **7.** $\begin{array}{r} 22 \\ -3 \\ \hline \end{array}$ **8.** $\begin{array}{r} 35 \\ -8 \\ \hline \end{array}$ **9.** $\begin{array}{r} 26 \\ -7 \\ \hline \end{array}$ **10.** $\begin{array}{r} 47 \\ -9 \\ \hline \end{array}$ **11.** $\begin{array}{r} 58 \\ -9 \\ \hline \end{array}$

$$\begin{array}{r} \overset{4}{\cancel{5}}\overset{11}{\cancel{2}}\overset{15}{\cancel{5}} \\ -86 \\ \hline 439 \end{array}$$ **12.** $\begin{array}{r} 431 \\ -63 \\ \hline \end{array}$ **13.** $\begin{array}{r} 352 \\ -74 \\ \hline \end{array}$ **14.** $\begin{array}{r} 234 \\ -55 \\ \hline \end{array}$ **15.** $\begin{array}{r} 655 \\ -66 \\ \hline \end{array}$ **16.** $\begin{array}{r} 286 \\ -98 \\ \hline \end{array}$

$$\begin{array}{r} \overset{7}{\cancel{8}}\overset{14}{\cancel{5}}\overset{13}{\cancel{3}} \\ -787 \\ \hline 66 \end{array}$$ **17.** $\begin{array}{r} 222 \\ 169 \\ \hline \end{array}$ **18.** $\begin{array}{r} 425 \\ 358 \\ \hline \end{array}$ **19.** $\begin{array}{r} 512 \\ -424 \\ \hline \end{array}$ **20.** $\begin{array}{r} 356 \\ -267 \\ \hline \end{array}$ **21.** $\begin{array}{r} 685 \\ -598 \\ \hline \end{array}$

$$\begin{array}{r} \overset{3}{\cancel{4}}\overset{9}{\cancel{0}}\overset{9}{\cancel{0}}\overset{10}{\cancel{0}} \\ -287 \\ \hline 3713 \end{array}$$ **22.** $\begin{array}{r} 300 \\ -23 \\ \hline \end{array}$ **23.** $\begin{array}{r} 5200 \\ -199 \\ \hline \end{array}$ **24.** $\begin{array}{r} 2005 \\ -576 \\ \hline \end{array}$ **25.** $\begin{array}{r} 1050 \\ -561 \\ \hline \end{array}$ **26.** $\begin{array}{r} 3020 \\ -342 \\ \hline \end{array}$

Checking the Difference

One way of checking your answer to a subtraction problem is to add the difference and the lower number. The sum should be equal to the larger number. Check your answers in this lesson, using this method.

$$\begin{array}{r} 1260 \\ -187 \\ \hline 1073 \end{array} \quad\times\quad \begin{array}{r} 1073 \\ +187 \\ \hline 1260 \end{array}$$

MULTIPLICATION OF WHOLE NUMBERS

To find the cost of 5 shirts at $6 each, you can add 6 + 6 + 6 + 6 + 6.
A quicker way is to multiply:

Which facts are missing? Put them where they belong.

0	1	2	3	4	5	6	7	8	9
0	1	2	3	4		6	7	8	9
×0	×0	×0	×0	×0		×0	×0	×0	×0
0	0	0	0	0		0	0	0	0
	1	2	3	4	5		7	8	9
	×1	×1	×1	×1	×1		×1	×1	×1
	1	2	3	4	5		7	8	9
0		2	3	4	5	6		8	9
×2		×2	×2	×2	×2	×2		×2	×2
0		4	6	8	10	12		16	18
0	1		3	4	5	6	7		9
×3	×3		×3	×3	×3	×3	×3		×3
0	3		9	12	15	18	21		27
0	1	2		4	5	6	7	8	
×4	×4	×4		×4	×4	×4	×4	×4	
0	4	8		16	20	24	28	32	
0	1	2	3		5	6	7		9
×5	×5	×5	×5		×5	×5	×5		×5
0	5	10	15		25	30	35		45
0	1	2		4	5	6		8	9
×6	×6	×6		×6	×6	×6		×6	×6
0	6	12		24	30	36		48	54
0	1		3	4	5		7	8	9
×7	×7		×7	×7	×7		×7	×7	×7
0	7		21	28	35		49	56	63
0		2	3	4		6	7	8	9
×8		×8	×8	×8		×8	×8	×8	×8
0		16	24	32		48	56	64	72
	1	2	3		5	6	7	8	9
	×9	×9	×9		×9	×9	×9	×9	×9
	9	18	27		45	54	63	72	81

MULTIPLICATION

As you work on real-life problems later on in this book, you may forget a few multiplication facts. Use this bank to help you remember.

Multiplying from Right to Left

How do you usually multiply 423 × 2?

A. Multiply, 3 × 2 = 6; write 6.

B. Multiply, 2 × 2 = 4; write 4 to the left of 6.

C. Multiply, 4 × 2 = 8; write 8 to the left of 4.

$$\begin{array}{r} 423 \\ \times\ 2 \\ \hline 846 \\ \text{CBA} \end{array}$$

Find the products.

1. $\begin{array}{r} 23 \\ \times\ 3 \\ \hline \end{array}$ **2.** $\begin{array}{r} 385 \\ \times\ 1 \\ \hline \end{array}$ **3.** $\begin{array}{r} 301 \\ \times\ 2 \\ \hline \end{array}$ **4.** $\begin{array}{r} 72 \\ \times\ 4 \\ \hline \end{array}$

5. $\begin{array}{r} 80 \\ \times\ 7 \\ \hline \end{array}$ **6.** $\begin{array}{r} 511 \\ \times\ 6 \\ \hline \end{array}$ **7.** $\begin{array}{r} 802 \\ \times\ 4 \\ \hline \end{array}$ **8.** $\begin{array}{r} 931 \\ \times\ 3 \\ \hline \end{array}$

Using Your Memory in Multiplication

How do you usually multiply 87 × 4?
Multiply, 7 × 4 = 28, write 8.

$$\begin{array}{r} 87 \\ \times 4 \\ \hline 8 \end{array}$$

Remember 2 from 28. Multiply, 8 × 4
= 32, add the remembered 2, 32 + 2 = 34;

Write 34 to the left of 8.

$$\begin{array}{r} 87 \\ \times 4 \\ \hline 348 \end{array}$$

Find the products.

9. $\begin{array}{r} 95 \\ \times\ 6 \\ \hline \end{array}$ **10.** $\begin{array}{r} 87 \\ \times\ 5 \\ \hline \end{array}$ **11.** $\begin{array}{r} 64 \\ \times\ 8 \\ \hline \end{array}$

12. $\begin{array}{r} 137 \\ \times\ 2 \\ \hline \end{array}$ **13.** $\begin{array}{r} 209 \\ \times\ 4 \\ \hline \end{array}$ **14.** $\begin{array}{r} 514 \\ \times\ 7 \\ \hline \end{array}$

Using Two Partial Products

To find 27 × 56, you often use the following method.

$$\begin{array}{r} 27 \\ \times 56 \\ \hline 162 \\ +135 \\ \hline 1512 \end{array}$$

162 ◄—— (27 × 6) partial product
+135 ◄—— (27 × 50) partial product
1512 ◄—— (162 + 1350) PRODUCT

Note: You do not have to write the 0 in 1350, because you will get the same product whether you write it or not.

Find the products.

15. $\begin{array}{r} 42 \\ \times 23 \\ \hline \end{array}$ **16.** $\begin{array}{r} 46 \\ \times 31 \\ \hline \end{array}$ **17.** $\begin{array}{r} 81 \\ \times 19 \\ \hline \end{array}$

18. $\begin{array}{r} 132 \\ \times\ 24 \\ \hline \end{array}$ **19.** $\begin{array}{r} 345 \\ \times\ 63 \\ \hline \end{array}$ **20.** $\begin{array}{r} 1213 \\ \times\ 32 \\ \hline \end{array}$

Using Three Partial Products

To find the product of 692 × 231 you often use the following method.

```
      692
     ×231
      692 ——(692 × 1) partial product
     2076 ——(692 × 30) partial product
   +1384   ——(692 × 200) partial product
   159852 ——PRODUCT
```

Find the products.

1. 765
×211

2. 348
×123

3. 879
×312

4. 647
×251

Zeros in Multiplication

Your solution to 225 × 304 may be written in two different ways.

First Method:

```
    225
   ×304
    900
    000
   +675
   68400
```

Second Method:

```
     225
   × 304
     900
     675
    68400
```

Use either method to find the products.

5. 352
×205

6. 864
×302

7. 506
×201

8. 708
×403

Multiplying by 10, 100, 1000

To multiply a number by 10, 100, or 1000, here's what you do.

$$35 \times 10 = 350$$

$$35 \times 100 = 3500$$

$$35 \times 1000 = 35000$$

Find the products.

9. 58 × 10 = ...

10. 58 × 100 = ...

11. 58 × 1000 = ...

12. 60 × 100 = ...

13. 45 × 10 = ...

14. 99 × 1000 = ...

15. 125 × 100 = ...

Checking Your Answers

One way of proving your product is to interchange the two numbers to be multiplied.

Check:

```
   43                15
  ×15               ×43
  215                45
  43                 60
  645 ——PRODUCT—— 645
```

Prove each product in Ex. 1-8.

How can you find the price of 1 record if 5 records cost $20? You can divide:

0	1	2	3	4	5	6	7	8	9
1)0	1)1	1)2	1)3		1)5		1)7	1)8	1)9
2)0	2)2	2)4		2)8	2)10	2)12		2)16	2)18
3)0	3)3		3)9	3)12	3)15	3)18	3)21		3)27
4)0		4)8	4)12	4)16	4)20	4)24	4)28	4)32	
	5)5	5)10	5)15	5)20		5)30	5)35		5)45
6)0		6)12	6)18	6)24	6)30	6)36		6)48	6)54
7)0	7)7		7)21	7)28	7)35		7)49	7)56	7)63
8)0	8)8	8)16		8)32		8)48	8)56	8)64	8)72
	9)9	9)18	9)27		9)45	9)54	9)63	9)72	

Which facts are missing? Put them where they belong.

You may forget some basic division facts as you work on real-life problems. Use this bank to help you remember

olving Division Problems

6 ÷ 23 is usually solved this way:

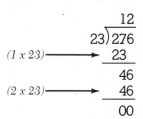

Find the quotients.

1. 9)828

2. 18)234

eros in the Quotient

e answer to 2461 ÷ 23 is sometimes incorrectly
itten as 17. It should be 107. To avoid this error,
u may write your work like this:

```
        107
   23)2461
       23
       16
       00
      161
      161
      000
```

Remember: Each time you bring down one digit from the dividend, you must write one digit in the quotient.

You may also avoid the mistake by estimating or guessing the quotient.

Estimate 2461 ÷ 23.

Round 2461 to 2000 and 23 to 20.

Since 2000 ÷ 20 = 100, you know that the quotient is about 100. So 17 is wrong.

nd the quotients.

3. 32)6592

4. 19)5795

5. 24)9696

6. 17)8534

hort Method of Dividing Rounded Numbers

multiplying 200 × 20, you simply write
ee zeros and multiply 2 × 2. Your answer
4000.

divide 4000 ÷ 200, this is what you do:

00 ÷ 200 = 40 ÷ 2 = 20

divide 8000 ÷ 4000:

00 ÷ 4000 = 8 ÷ 4 = 2

Find the quotients.

7. 6000 ÷ 2000 = ...

8. 4500 ÷ 900 = ...

9. 3500 ÷ 700 = ...

10. 800 ÷ 200 = ...

1. Write a simple rule for dividing rounded numbers. ....

What will be the first digit in each quotient?

1. 40)1728   48)1728

2. 70)3672   72)3672

3. 20)1152   24)1152

Check if each answer is reasonable.

4.
$$\begin{array}{r} 47 \\ 35\overline{)1645} \end{array}$$
....

5.
$$\begin{array}{r} 57 \\ 71\overline{)4047} \end{array}$$
....

6.
$$\begin{array}{r} 34 \\ 27\overline{)8208} \end{array}$$
....

Find each quotient.

7. 72)3672   **8.** 24)1152

Remainders in Division

To change minutes to hours, you divide the number of minutes by 60. (60 min. = 1 hr.) Sometimes there are leftover minutes. In division, these leftovers are called remainders.

135 min. ÷ 60 = ?

The answer is 2 hours and 15 minutes.

$$\begin{array}{r} 2 \\ 60\overline{)135} \\ 120 \\ \hline 15 \end{array} \longleftarrow Remainder$$

Find the quotients and the remainders.

9. 198 min. ÷ 60 = ... hr. .... min.

10. 56 inches ÷ 12 = ... feet .... inch

11. 86 days ÷ 24 = ... days .... hour

12. 556 ounces ÷ 16 = ... pounds .... our

ESTIMATING

Guessing the Answer

"Do I have enough money?" How often do you ask this to yourself just before going to the cashier? You can find a quick, reasonable answer by **estimating**—guessing a fairly close answer to a math problem.

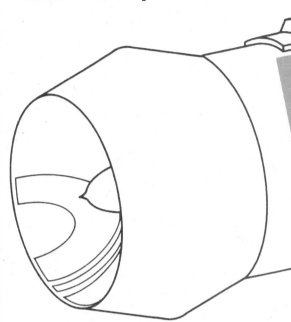

FACT BOX The question to be answered often tells you how to estimate. For example, here are two different questions about the same ad. The estimates are done in different ways.

What is the cost of 2 batteries?

Step 1: Round 78¢ to 80¢.

Step 2: Figure 80 + 80 or 80 x 2 to guess the answer—about $1.60.

Is $1.60 enough to buy 2 batteries?

Step 1: Figure, $1.60 ÷ 2 = 80¢

Step 2: Think, since 78¢ is about 80¢, the answer is most likely to be yes.

FLASHLIGHT BATTERIES 78¢ each

You may have your own ways of estimating. Here's a chance for you to use them. Look at the facts in each ad. Quickly guess the answer to each question and circle it. Don't do any figuring on paper.

BUTTONS 29¢ each

1. How much will 2 buttons cost?

About 60¢   About 40¢

2. Is 90¢ enough to buy 3 buttons?

Yes   No

3. Suppose you buy 1 button. How much change will you get out of 50¢?

About 30¢   About 20¢

CASSETTES 3 FOR $5

4. How much does each cassette cost?

About $1   About $2

5. Can you buy 2 cassettes for $4?

Yes   No

6. How many cassettes can $12 buy?

6   7   8

Checking Answers by Estimating

By guessing the answer to a problem, you have a way of checking if your actual answer is right or wrong. For example, if your estimate is 1000 and your actual answer is 110, you know that you made a mistake somewhere. You can then do the problem again.

One common method used to estimate answers in math problems is to round numbers to the nearest ten, hundred, or thousand so that you can work with them mentally.
To estimate 898 + 204, for example:

$$
\begin{array}{ll}
898 & \text{is rounded to} \quad 900 \\
\underline{+204} & \text{is rounded to} \quad \underline{+200} \\
\end{array}
$$

Sum ⟶ 1102   1100 ⟵ Estimate

Estimate the sums.

1. 813 + 692: .... + ... = ...

2. 3185 + 1812: .... + ... = ...

3. 62 + 78 + 39: .... + ... + ... = ...

Estimate the differences.

4. 706 − 598: .... − .... = ...

5. 497 − 208: .... − .... = ...

6. 6028 − 3982: .... − .... = ...

Estimate the products.

7. 29 × 31: .... × .... = ...

8. 88 × 52: .... × .... = ...

9. 394 × 203: .... × .... = ...

Estimate the quotients.

10. 4105 ÷ 79: .... ÷ .... = ...

11. 2950 ÷ 51: .... ÷ .... = ...

KILLS SURVEY

nate the answers before solving the math problems below.

	56 +41	**2.**	352 + 26	**3.**	263 +715	**4.**	2136 +4041
	35 + 6	**6.**	48 +25	**7.**	507 +197	**8.**	726 +384

up the addends and find the sums.

42 + 200 + 2312 + 3 = ?

10. 4 + 7201 + 33 + 120 = ?

ract.

	48 −17	**12.**	352 − 85	**13.**	6000 − 134	**14.**	3060 − 483

iply.

	32 × 3	**16.**	602 × 2	**17.**	75 × 4	**18.**	412 × 7
	24 ×32	**20.**	253 × 26	**21.**	531 ×213	**22.**	304 ×502

de.

. 32)384   **24.** 8)776   **25.** 26)7904   **26.** 4500 ÷ 90 = ...

t are the four basic operations you used to solve the problems on this page?

: ....   **28.** ....

: ....   **30.** ....

21

YOU'RE ON YOUR WAY!

Where does all the money go? How much do I have to save to buy that car? How can I earn more? Which cost is the better buy? What's the score?
You can now use your math skills to answer these questions, and more.

ou end every
k with the words,
ere has all the
ey gone?" If you
ver "Yes," this
is for you.

YOUR DAILY
EXPENSES

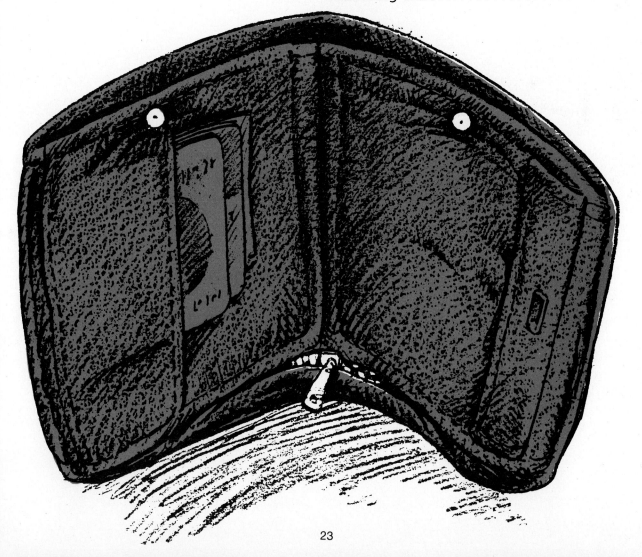

Menu

Hot Specials

Hamburger.	$2.45
Cheeseburger.	2.65
Chopped Steak.	3.50
Fried Shrimp.	4.25
Broiled Filet of Sole.	4.50
Seafood Platter.	5.25

SIDE ORDERS

Soup of the Day.	$.75
Salad with Dressing.	.80
Vegetable.	.55
Cole Slaw.	.35
Onion Rings.	.50
French Fries.	.55
Baked Potato.	.50

SANDWICHES

Egg Salad.	$2.50
Tuna.	2.95
Turkey.	3.25
Chicken Salad.	2.75
Ham & Cheese.	2.95
Roast Beef.	3.50

DESSERTS

Chocolate Cake.	$.65
Apple Pie.	.79
Cheesecake.	.85
Ice Cream Scoop.	.75
Donut.	.35

Beverages

Fruit Juice.	$.55	Hot Chocolate.	.65
Milk.	.50	Coffee or Tea.	.60

Paying for a Meal

Plan ahead...How much cash do you have? In most problems involving money, **addition** is the key. The prices of what you order should add up to the total amount you pay. This lesson provides practice in finding the total cost of a meal.

FACT BOX

When adding money, remember these steps:

Line up the amounts so that the decimal points are directly under each other.

Add each column of numbers from right to left.

The **sum**, or **total**, is the answer to an addition problem.

To check each answer, add the amounts again, starting with a different number first.

Look at the menu to find the price of each item. Write the prices and then add to find the total cost of each meal. Ex. 1 is done for you.

1. Hamburger $2.45

Hot Chocolate .... .65

Total $3.10

2. Tuna Sandwich ....

Soup ....

Apple Pie ....

Total ....

3. Ham & Cheese Sandwich ....

Milk ....

Total ....

4. Cheeseburger ....

Fruit Juice ....

Total ....

5. Roast Beef Sandwich ....

French Fries ....

Hot Chocolate ....

Total ....

6. Fried Shrimp ....

Onion Rings ....

Tea ....

Total ....

7. Chicken Salad Sandwich ....

Soup ....

Apple Pie ....

Total ....

8. Turkey Sandwich ....

Cole Slaw ....

Fruit Juice ....

Total ....

9. Seafood Platter ....

Vegetable ....

Cheesecake ....

Coffee ....

Total ....

10. Chopped Steak ....

Baked Potato ....

Chocolate Cake ....

Tea ....

Total ....

11. Filet of Sole ....

French Fries ....

Salad with Dressing ....

Fruit Juice ....

Total ....

ON YOUR OWN

Now list the items that you would like to order. Compute the total cost of your meal.

....

....

....

....

Total ....

How often do you say, "Where has all the money gone?" This lesson, which uses continuous subtraction, will help you keep track of your expenses.

Complete this week's calendar of expenses. Subtract the expense, or amount paid, from the balance. Write the difference on the new balance line.

$$ EXPENS[E]

	SUNDAY		MONDAY		TUESDAY
Start-of-Day Balance		$150.00		$138.78	
Expense	Bus Fare	1.50	Train Ticket	10.00	Photo Prints
New Balance		148.50			
Expense	Contribution	1.00	Breakfast	1.39	Film
New Balance		147.50			
Expense	Laundry	3.60	Records	5.72	Lunch
New Balance		143.90			
Expense	Newspaper	.75	Health Aids	4.08	Light Bulbs
New Balance		143.15			
Expense	Ball Game	2.50	Watch Repair	5.63	Picture Frame
New Balance		140.65			
Expense	Snack	1.87	Magazine	1.25	String
New Balance		138.78			
Expense					Cleaners
New Balance					
Expense					
End-of-Day Balance		$138.78			

To check each answer, add the difference and
the amount subtracted. The sum should be the same
as the original amount. Study this example:

150.00 original amount	$148.50
1.50 amount subtracted	+ 1.50
148.50 difference	$150.00

Keep track of your Saturday expenses. Write the
amount of money you have on the first line. Subtract each expense. How much do you have at
the end of the day?

ALENDAR $$

WEDNESDAY		THURSDAY		FRIDAY		SATURDAY
Sweater	6.99	Groceries	11.83	Newspapers	1.20	
Jeans	12.98	Legal Pad	.67	Gift	3.87	
T-Shirt	5.27	Notebook	.74	Flowers	1.25	
Sneakers	8.36	Pen	1.37	Plant	4.99	
Snack	.91	Paperback	1.08	Vase	3.25	
Gym Fee	1.50			Concert Tickets	7.00	
				Cab Fare	2.35	
				Dinner	7.90	

(Unit Price × Quantity) + Sales Tax

6% SALES TAX CHART							
Amount of Sale	Tax	Amount of Sale	Tax	Amount of Sale	Tax	Amount of Sale	Tax
$.00— .10	none	$2.35—2.50	.15	$5.11— 5.17	.31	$7.68— 7.84	.47
.11— .17	.01	2.51—2.67	.16	5.18— 5.34	.32	7.85— 8.10	.48
.18— .34	.02	2.68—2.84	.17	5.35— 5.50	.33	8.11— 8.17	.49
.35— .50	.03	2.85—3.10	.18	5.51— 5.67	.34	8.18— 8.34	.50
.51— .67	.04	3.11—3.17	.19	5.68— 5.84	.35	8.35— 8.50	.51
.68— .84	.05	3.18—3.34	.20	5.85— 6.10	.36	8.51— 8.67	.52
.85—1.10	.06	3.35—3.50	.21	6.11— 6.17	.37	8.68— 8.84	.53
1.11—1.17	.07	3.51—3.67	.22	6.18— 6.34	.38	8.85— 9.10	.54
1.18—1.34	.08	3.68—3.84	.23	6.35— 6.50	.39	9.11— 9.17	.55
1.35—1.50	.09	3.85—4.10	.24	6.51— 6.67	.40	9.18— 9.34	.56
1.51—1.67	.10	4.11—4.17	.25	6.68— 6.84	.41	9.35— 9.50	.57
1.68—1.84	.11	4.18—4.34	.26	6.85— 7.10	.42	9.51— 9.67	.58
1.85—2.10	.12	4.35—4.50	.27	7.11— 7.17	.43	9.68— 9.84	.59
2.11—2.17	.13	4.51—4.67	.28	7.18— 7.34	.44	9.85—10.00	.60
2.18—2.34	.14	4.68—4.84	.29	7.35— 7.50	.45		
		4.85—5.10	.30	7.51— 7.67	.46		

 Have you ever been surprised that the bill for a $10.00 item is $10.60? This lesson will help you understand sales tax and how it affects the amount a customer pays.

 On each sales receipt, find the total cost of the items described. Add the amounts in the total-cost column to find the subtotal. Use the Sales Tax Chart to determine the tax on the subtotal. Add the subtotal and the tax to find the final amount due from the customer. Ex. 1 has been completed for you.

FACT BOX

✳ **Quantity** or **Qty.** is the number of items purchased or bought.

✳ **Unit Price** is the cost of one item.

✳ **Total Cost** is Unit Price × Quantity.

✳ The answer in multiplication is called the **product.**

✳ **Subtotal** is the sum of the amounts in the total-cost column before the sales tax is added.

✳ **6% Sales Tax** means an addition of $.06 on each dollar of purchase. (Many states and cities raise money through sales taxes. The customer pays the tax in the store.)

✳ To use the **Sales Tax Chart,** find the subtotal ($5.33) within the two amounts ($5.18-$5.34) shown in the amount-of-sale columns. The sales tax (.32) is at the right of these two columns.

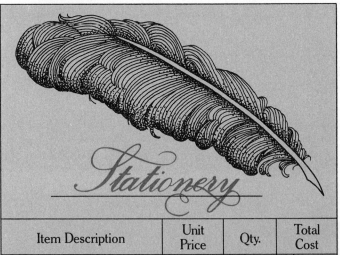

Stationery

Item Description	Unit Price	Qty.	Total Cost
Pens	.79	3	$2.37
Memo Pads	.39	5	1.95
Scotch Tape	.41	1	.41
Pencils	.15	4	.60
		Subtotal	$5.33
		6% Tax	.32
		Pay this amount	$5.65

$ .79
× 3
$2.37

$ .39
× 5
$1.95

$.41
× 1
$.41

$.15
× 4
$.60

◄—— Sum of the amounts in Total-Cost column.

◄—— Tax for $5.33 as shown on Sales Tax chart.

◄—— Sum of Subtotal and Sales Tax.

28

Alan's Camera Supply

Item Description	Unit Price	Qty.	Total Cost
Film	2.79	2	
Color Prints	.28	12	
Flash Cubes	.32	6	
Slides	.14	12	
	Subtotal		
	6% Tax		
	Pay this amount		

SEWING NOTIONS

Item Description	Unit Price	Qty.	Total Cost
Fabric (Yards)	4.98	2	
Buttons	.20	10	
Needles	.08	6	
Spools of Thread	.80	3	
Patterns	2.50	2	
	Subtotal		
	6% Tax		
	Pay this amount		

BULBS & PLANTS

Item Description	Unit Price	Qty.	Total Cost
Seed Packets	.18	12	
Bags of Soil	1.79	2	
Plant Food (Boxes)	.49	4	
Pots	.15	3	
	Subtotal		
	6% Tax		
	Pay this amount		

ACE HARDWARE

Item Description	Unit Price	Qty.	Total Cost
Nails	.07	22	
Screws	.09	16	
Pine Wood	.88	4	
Tape Measure	1.76	1	
Glue	.54	2	
	Subtotal		
	6% Tax		
	Pay this amount		

ON YOUR OWN

Make a receipt of some things you bought recently. What did you buy? How many? How much did each one cost? How much tax was included in the total amount you paid?

Item Description	Unit Price	Qty.	Total Cost
	Subtotal		
	Tax		
	Pay this amount		

DIFFERENT STATES, DIFFERENT PERCENT

 Sales tax percents vary from state to state as you can see on the map. Some cities also require additional sales taxes. In this lesson, however, you will use only the state sales tax to see how different rates affect the final cost of an item.

 Study the steps taken to answer Ex. 1. Then complete Ex. 2-6.

1. What is 2% of $4.00?

Step A: $2\% = 2.\%$
$= .02$
$2\% = .02$

Step B: $\begin{array}{r} \$4.00 \\ \times\ .02 \\ \hline \$.0800 \end{array}$

Step C: 2% of $\$4.00 = \$.08$

2. What is 3% of $25.00? ....

3. What is 4% of $666.00? ....

4. What is 5% of $7.00? ....

5. What is 6% of $16.00? ....

6. What is 7% of $8.00? ....

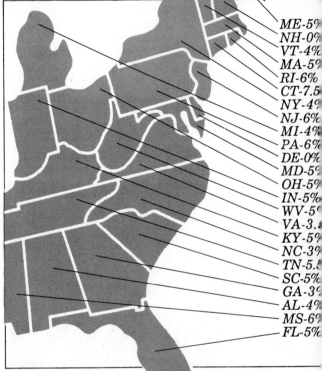

ME-5%
NH-0%
VT-4%
MA-5%
RI-6%
CT-7.5
NY-4%
NJ-6%
MI-4%
PA-6%
DE-0%
MD-5%
OH-5%
IN-5%
WV-5%
VA-3.
KY-5%
NC-3%
TN-5.
SC-5%
GA-3%
AL-4%
MS-6%
FL-5%

 Round each answer to the nearest cent.
7 is done for you.

If the third decimal place is less than 5, the seco
decimal place remains the same. If it is 5 or more, a
1 to the second decimal place.

7. $\begin{array}{r} \$765.01 \\ \times\ .07 \\ \hline \$53.5507 \end{array}$ = $53.5

8. $\begin{array}{r} \$521.35 \\ \times\ .03 \\ \hline \end{array}$ = ...

9. $\begin{array}{r} \$\ 62.93 \\ \times\ .06 \\ \hline \end{array}$ = ...

10. $\begin{array}{r} \$3999.99 \\ \times\ .04 \\ \hline \end{array}$ = ...

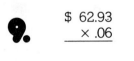

FACT BOX

To find a percent of an amount:

✪ Change the percent to a decimal.

✪ Drop the percent sign.

✪ Move the decimal point 2 places to the left of its original position.

$3\% = 3.\%$
$= .03$
$3\% = .03$

✪ Multiply the amount by the decimal.

$\begin{array}{ll} \$4.00 & \text{2 decimal places} \\ \underline{\times\ .03} & \text{2 decimal places} \\ \$.1200 & \text{4 decimal places} \end{array}$

Use the map to find the percent of sales tax in each state listed. Find the after-tax cost of the same item in different states. Ex. 1 is done for you.

1. You purchase a taxable item which costs $.58.

STATE	SALES TAX IN %	SALES TAX AS DECIMAL	AMOUNT OF TAX	TOTAL PURCHASE PRICE
RHODE ISLAND	6%	.06	.06 x .58 = .0348 = .03	.58 + .03 = $.61
NEW YORK	4%	.04	.04 x .58 = .0232 = .02	.58 + .02 = $.60
GEORGIA	3%	.03	.03 x .58 = .0174 = .02	.58 + .02 = $.60

2. You purchase a taxable item which costs $6.99.

STATE	SALES TAX IN %	SALES TAX AS DECIMAL	AMOUNT OF TAX	TOTAL PURCHASE PRICE
CONNECTICUT				
NORTH CAROLINA				
MAINE				

3. What is the difference in price in Pennsylvania and Mississippi on a taxable item which costs $42.50?

STATE	SALES TAX IN %	SALES TAX AS DECIMAL	AMOUNT OF TAX	TOTAL PURCHASE PRICE
OHIO				
PENNSYLVANIA				

The difference between the two prices is ....

4. What is the difference in price in Indiana and Connecticut on a taxable item which costs $345.99?

STATE	SALES TAX IN %	SALES TAX AS DECIMAL	AMOUNT OF TAX	TOTAL PURCHASE PRICE
INDIANA				
CONNECTICUT				

The difference between the two prices is ....

HOW TO SAVE ON TRANSPORTATION

 One-way fare? Monthly ticket? Weekly rate? Which is the best buy? This lesson will show yo that the number of trips you take affects which fare plan is best for you.

 The people in the following exercises are commuters or regular riders on the Long Island Ra road. Decide how much they pay on one-way trips for each fare plan shown on the chart. Ex. is done for you.

THE LONG ISLAND RAILROAD

LOCATION	MONTHLY	WEEKLY	REGULAR ONE-WAY
BABYLON	112.00	35.00	5.00
RONKONKOMA	132.00	41.00	6.00
HOLTSVILLE	143.00	44.00	6.75
BELLPORT	160.00	50.00	7.75
GREENPORT	175.00	54.00	10.50
MONTAUK	175.00	54.00	10.50

Jamaica to

MONTHLY: Good for 60 one-way trips for a month   WEEKLY: Good for 14 one-way trips for a week
REGULAR ONE-WAY: Good for 1 one-way trip

1. Dr. Jack Spenser goes to Babylon and returns home to Jamaica 3 times a week for one month.

a. What does the regular one-way ticket cost? $5.00   from the chart under Regular One-Way

b. How many one-way trips does he make in one week?   6

```
  2 trips a day
× 3 days a week
  6 trips a week
```

c. How much is a weekly ticket? $35.00

d. What is the cost of each trip on the weekly fare plan? $5.83

```
  6 trips a week
× 4 weeks a month
 24 trips a month
```

```
      5.833  rounded
  6)35.000   to $5.
    30
    50
    48
    20
    18
     2
```

e. How many one-way trips does he make in one month?   24

f. How much is a monthly ticket? $112.00

g. What is the cost of each trip on the monthly fare plan? $4.67 👉

    4.666 rounded to $4.67
24)112.000
   96
   160
   144
   160
   144
   160
   144
    16

h. Which fare plan is cheaper for Dr. Spenser?   .... monthly ....

2. Pat goes to Jamaica and back home to Bell-port 5 times a week for a month.

a. What does the regular one-way ticket cost?   ....

b. How many one-way trips does Pat make in a week?   ....

c. How much does a weekly ticket cost?   ....

d. What is the cost of each trip on the weekly fare plan?   ....

e. How many one-way trips are made in a month?   ....

f. How much is a monthly ticket?   ....

g. What is the cost of each trip on the monthly fare plan?   ....

h. Which fare plan is cheapest?   ....

3. Steve makes 14 one-way trips a week between Jamaica and Greenport.

a. How much is the regular one-way ticket?   ....

b. What is the cost of each trip on a weekly ticket?   ....

c. How much will Steve save if he buys the weekly ticket? (Subtract answer b from answer a.)   ....

ON YOUR OWN

Pick a place where you might go to work regularly. Ask your local bus company or railroad about special fare plans. Decide which plan is best for you.

Regular one-way fare   ....

Monthly rate   ....

Number of trips you might make in a month   ....

Cost of each one-way trip   ....

Weekly rate   ....

Number of trips you might make in a week   ....

Cost of each one-way trip   ....

AT THE GROCERY

Golden Corn
4 10-oz. Cans **$1.00**

Navel Oranges

Juicy Sweet **12** for **$1.10**

Watermelon	**$2.50** ea.
Pineapple	**1.00** ea.
Cantaloupe	**.79** ea.

FRESH GRADE A
MEAT

Beef Roasts	**$1.49/lb.**
Pork Chops	**1.39/lb.**
Frying Chickens	**.69/lb.**
Turkeys	**.69/lb.**

Cooked Shrimp.	1 lb.	$2.65
Fried Fish.	1 lb.	.99
Fresh Perch.	1 lb.	1.49

FACT BOX

○ A fraction is a part of a whole.

○ **To find a fractional cost:** Multiply the cost of the whole item by the numerator of the fraction. Then divide the result by the denominator.

$$\frac{1}{2} \times \$1.50 = \frac{1.50}{2}$$

$$\frac{1.50}{2} = 2\overline{)1.50} = \$.75$$
$$\begin{array}{r} .75 \\ 2\overline{)1.50} \\ \underline{1.4} \\ 10 \\ \underline{10} \\ 00 \end{array}$$

1 whole   *3/4 three fourths or three quarters*   *1/2 one half*   *1/4 one fourth or one quarter*

 "I can't believe I have to buy the WHOLE thing!" What if you only want to buy a quarter of a watermelon or half a pound of pork chops? To figure out the cost of anything less than the whole item, you have to use fractions.

 Use the advertised prices to compute the total cost of each shopping list. Often you must figure the fractional cost of an item. Ex. 1 is done and explained for you.

34

1.
$\frac{1}{2}$ watermelon .... $1.25 ← $\frac{1}{2}$ of $2.50 = \frac{2.50}{2} = 2\overline{)2.50}^{1.25}$

1 can of corn .... .25 ← $\frac{1}{4}$ of $1.00 = \frac{1.00}{4} = 4\overline{)1.00}^{.25}$

1 lb. turkey .... .69 ← from the ad

Total $2.19

2. 1 pineapple ....

1 lb. chicken ....

$\frac{1}{3}$ lb. fried fish ....

Total ....

3. 1 lb. beef roast ....

$\frac{3}{4}$ watermelon ....

$\frac{1}{2}$ lb. shrimp ....

Total ....

4. $\frac{1}{3}$ lb. perch ....

$\frac{1}{2}$ pineapple ....

3 cans corn ....

Total ....

5. 2 cans corn ....

6 oranges ....

$\frac{2}{3}$ lb. chicken ....

$\frac{1}{4}$ lb. pork chops ....

Total ....

6. $\frac{1}{5}$ lb. shrimp ....

1 cantaloupe ....

$\frac{2}{5}$ watermelon ....

$\frac{2}{3}$ lb. turkey ....

Total ....

7. 12 oranges ....

$\frac{1}{2}$ lb. fried fish ....

$\frac{3}{4}$ lb. beef roast ....

$\frac{2}{3}$ watermelon ....

Total ....

8. $\frac{1}{2}$ lb. pork chops ....

$\frac{2}{3}$ lb. fried fish ....

$\frac{1}{2}$ lb. shrimp ....

4 oranges ....

$\frac{1}{2}$ pineapple ....

Total ....

9. 3 oranges ....

1 cantaloupe ....

$\frac{1}{4}$ lb. perch ....

$\frac{3}{4}$ lb. turkey ....

$\frac{1}{2}$ lb. beef roast ....

Total ....

ON YOUR OWN

List the things you want to buy. Compute the total cost of your list.

....

....

....

....

....

....

....

....

CALLS TO:	STATION-TO-STATION										PERSON-TO-PERSON			
	DIRECT-DISTANCE DIALED						OPERATOR-ASSISTED							
	FULL WEEKDAY RATE Mon.-Fri. 8 AM-5 PM		EVENING Sun.-Fri. 5 PM-11 PM		NIGHT & WEEKEND Every Night 11 PM—8 AM All Day and Night on Sat. to 5 PM Sun.		ALL DAYS & HOURS	WEEKDAYS 8 AM-5 PM	EVENING Sun.-Fri. 5 PM-11 PM	NIGHT & WEEKEND Every Night 11 PM—8 AM All Day and Night on Sat. to 5 PM Sun.	ALL DAYS & HOURS	WEEKDAYS 8 AM-5 PM	EVENING Sun.-Fri. 5 PM-11 PM	NIGHT & WEEKEND Every Night 11 PM—8 A All Day an Night on S to 5 PM Su
	Init. 1 Min.	Ea. Add. Min.	Init. 1 Min.	Ea. Add. Min.	Init. 1 Min.	Ea. Add. Min.	Init. 3 Mins.	Ea. Add. Min.	Ea. Add. Min.	Ea. Add. Min.	Init. 3 Mins.	Ea. Add. Min.	Ea. Add. Min.	Ea. Add. Min.
Atlanta, Ga.	.50	.34	.33	.22	.20	.14	2.05	.34	.22	.14	3.15	.34	.22	.14
Atlantic City, N.J.	.43	.28	.28	.18	.17	.11	1.75	.28	.18	.11	2.75	.28	.18	.11
Boston, Mass.	.44	.29	.29	.19	.18	.12	1.85	.29	.19	.12	2.85	.29	.19	.12
Chicago, Ill.	.50	.34	.33	.22	.20	.14	2.05	.34	.22	.14	3.15	.34	.22	.14
Cleveland, Ohio	.48	.33	.31	.21	.19	.13	2.00	.33	.21	.13	3.05	.33	.21	.13
Denver, Colo.	.52	.36	.34	.23	.21	.14	2.15	.36	.23	.14	3.30	.36	.23	.14
Detroit, Mich.	.50	.34	.33	.22	.20	.14	2.05	.34	.22	.14	3.15	.34	.22	.14
Hartford, Conn.	.43	.28	.28	.18	.17	.11	1.75	.28	.18	.11	2.75	.28	.18	.11
Houston, Tex.	.52	.36	.34	.23	.21	.14	2.15	.36	.23	.14	3.30	.36	.23	.14
Los Angeles, Cal.	.54	.38	.35	.25	.22	.15	2.25	.38	.25	.15	3.55	.38	.25	.15
Miami, Fla.	.52	.36	.34	.23	.21	.14	2.15	.36	.23	.14	3.30	.36	.23	.14
Milwaukee, Wisc.	.50	.34	.33	.22	.20	.14	2.05	.34	.22	.14	3.15	.34	.22	.14
New Orleans, La.	.52	.36	.34	.23	.21	.14	2.15	.36	.23	.14	3.30	.36	.23	.14
Philadelphia, Pa.	.43	.28	.28	.18	.17	.11	1.75	.28	.18	.11	2.75	.28	.18	.11
Portland, Maine	.46	.31	.30	.20	.18	.12	1.95	.31	.20	.12	2.95	.31	.20	.12
St. Louis, Mo.	.50	.34	.33	.22	.20	.14	2.05	.34	.22	.14	3.15	.34	.22	.14
Seattle, Wash.	.54	.38	.35	.25	.22	.15	2.25	.38	.25	.15	3.55	.38	.25	.15
Washington, D.C.	.46	.31	.30	.20	.18	.12	1.95	.31	.20	.12	2.95	.31	.20	.12
Wilmington, Del.	.43	.28	.28	.18	.17	.11	1.75	.28	.18	.11	2.75	.28	.18	.11

FACT BOX

- **Station-to-Station**—time begins as soon as someone answers the number called

- **Person-to-Person**—time begins only when the specific person called is on the line

- **Direct-Distance Dialed (area code + local number)**—calls in which the caller dials the number directly without help from an operator

- **Operator-Assisted (0 + area code + local number)**—calls which require the operator's help to complete

- **Init.**—initial or beginning minutes

- **Ea. Add. Min.**—each additional minute

Is long-distance really the next best thing to being there? Many companies provide long-distance telephone service. Rates vary widely. You can practice using this chart to compute the cost of long-distance calls from one city. It's your choice: station-to-station, person-to-person, direct-dialing, operator assisted, day or night. Maybe you'll decide that being there is the only thing!

Use the chart to find the cost of the following calls. Ex. 1 is done for you.

1. To Portland, Maine, person-to-person, on Thursday at 8:00 P.M., for 13 minutes

Init. 3 mins. .... $2.95 ←——— from the chart

Add. 10 mins. .... 2.00 ←——

Total cost .... 4.95 ←——

10 mins.
× .20 for each additional minute
$2.00

$2.95
+2.00
$4.95

2. To Los Angeles, California, operator-assisted, on Friday at 10:00 P.M. for 7 minutes

Init. 3 mins. ....

Add. 4 mins. ....

Total cost ....

3. To Washington, D.C., direct-distance dialed, on Wednesday at 9:00 P.M., for 30 minutes

Init. 1 min. ....

Add. 29 mins. ....

Total cost ....

4. What is the difference in cost between the following two calls?
a. To St. Louis, Missouri, person-to-person, on Wednesday at 8:00 A.M. for 9 minutes

Init. 3 mins. ....

Add. 6 mins. ....

Total cost ....

b. To St. Louis, Missouri, direct-distance dialed, on Wednesday at 8:00 A.M. for 9 minutes

Init. 1 min. ....

Add. 8 mins. ....

Total cost ....

The difference in cost ....

5. What is the difference in cost between the following two calls?
a. To Denver, Colorado, direct-distance dialed, on Sunday at 3:00 P.M., for 22 minutes

Init. 1 min. ....

Add. 21 mins. ....

Total cost ....

b. To Denver, Colorado, operator-assisted, on Sunday at 3:00 P.M., for 22 minutes

Init. 3 mins. ....

Add. 19 mins. ....

Total cost ....

The difference in cost ....

ON YOUR OWN

Make up your own chart of long-distance calls. List the cities you want to call and find the total cost of each call.

City Called	Type of Call	Time Called	Minutes	Total Cost

In the Post Office

Maybe sending a letter is the next best thing to being there. Wait till you see how much it costs! Many post offices provide scales so that you can weigh your own mail and figure its cost. This lesson will give you practice in reading scales and figuring the cost of first-class, second-class, and third-class mailings.

Write the weight shown on the scale for each letter A-F. Then compute the mailing cost of a first-class rate of $.25 for the first ounce (oz.) or fraction of an ounce and $.20 for each additional ounce or fraction up to 11 oz. Letter D is done for you.

First Class Mail: Written letters and other sealed matter may be sent by first-class mail.

Letter	Weight	Cost of 1st Oz. or Fraction	Cost of Additional Oz. or Fraction	Total Cost
a				
b				
c				
d	$8\frac{1}{4}$ oz.	$.25	$8\frac{1}{4}$ oz. − 1st. oz. = $7\frac{1}{4}$ oz. $8 \times \$.20 = \$1.60$	$.25 + $1.60 = $1.85
e				
f				

Priority Mail: Items that are too heavy to send by first-class mail may be sent by priority mail. The cost depends on what zone the item, up to 70 pounds, is being mailed to.

 Use the table to determine the mailing cost of G–L at priority-class rate to the zone indicated.

Weight	Zones					
up to but not over	Local 1, 2, and 3	4	5	6	7	8
2 lb.	$2.40	$2.40	$2.40	$2.40	$2.40	$2.40
3	2.74	3.16	3.45	3.74	3.96	4.32
4	3.18	3.75	4.13	4.53	4.92	5.33
5	3.61	4.32	4.86	5.27	5.81	6.37
10	5.85	7.39	8.44	9.44	10.45	11.70
15	7.97	10.28	11.86	13.36	14.87	16.75
20	10.09	13.17	15.27	17.27	19.29	21.79
70	31.29	42.07	49.47	56.47	63.49	72.24

Mail	Weight	Zone	Total Cost
g	15½ oz.	7	
h	3 lb.	3	
i	70 lb.	8	
j	4 lb. 2 oz.	1	
k	20 lb.	5	
l	1 lb. 4 oz.	4	

Third-Class Mail: Greeting cards, printed matter, small parcels, booklets, and catalogs weighing less than 16 ounces may be mailed third class.

 Write the weight shown on the scale for each mailing M–R. Find the mailing cost, using this rate information:

```
0 to 1 oz.   ............................   .25
Over 1 to 2 oz.   .........................   .45
Over 2 to 3 oz.   .........................   .65
Over 3 to 4 oz.   .........................   .85
Over 4 to 6 oz.   .........................  1.00
Over 6 to 8 oz.   .........................  1.10
Over 8 to 10 oz.   ........................  1.20
Over 10 to 12 oz.   .......................  1.30
Over 12 to 14 oz.   .......................  1.40
Over 14 to 15.99 oz.   ....................  1.50
```

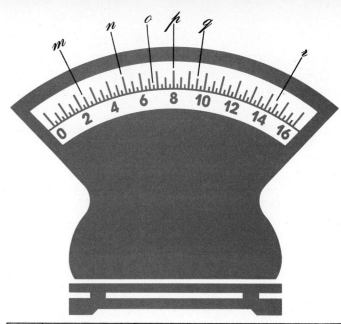

Mail	Weight	Total Cost
m		
n		
o		
p		
q		
r	14 ¼ oz.	$1.50

ON YOUR OWN

Packages weighing 16 ounces or more, but not more than 40 lb., may be mailed by parcel post or fourth-class mail. Rates are based on weight but they also vary according to distance. Next time you mail packages to friends or relatives, ask for the rates at the parcel-post window in your post office. Use this chart to record the cost of the packages you send.

To Whom	Where	Weight	Cost

LOOKING BACK

1. Write a check for one dinner that includes the following: shrimp cocktail—$2.35, steak—$6.66, apple pie—$.75, and tea—$.30. Add 5% sales tax. Compute the total bill.

CAFÉ

Menu Item	Price
Subtotal	
Tax	
Total	

Thank You-Call Again!

2. Your cash balance on Monday morning was $100.00. Your expenses from Monday to Friday were: $28.50, $6.88, $32.69, $17.34, and $10.25. How much money did you have at the end of each day? What was your end-of-week balance?

Balance
Monday Expenses
New Balance
Tuesday Expenses
New Balance
Wednesday Expenses
New Balance
Thursday Expenses
New Balance
Friday Expenses
End-of-Week Balance
☺ SATURDAY ☺

3. Fill out a sales receipt for 3 pens—$.39 each, 1 legal pad—$.50 each, 2 notebooks—$.75 each, and 4 pencils—$.05 each. Include 8% sales tax. Compute the total receipt.

PAD & PENCIL SUPPLY CO.

Item Description	Unit Price	Qty.	Total Cost
	Subtotal		
	Tax		
	Pay this amount		

4. How much will a $.69 item cost with sales tax in the following four cities?

Toronto 8% ....
New York City 8.25% ....
San Francisco 6.25% ....
Houston 7.25% ....

5. A monthly ticket which is good for 60 trips costs $143.00. A weekly ticket valid for 14 trips costs $44.00. The regular one-way fare is $6.75. Which ticket should the following people buy?

a. Suzie Tan who makes 42 trips a month:

....

b. Felix Santos who goes to work and returns home 3 times a week.

....

6. A sack of rice costs $14.70. Write the cost of each fractional part of the sack.

$\frac{3}{4}$ ....

$\frac{2}{3}$ ....

$\frac{1}{2}$ ....

$\frac{1}{3}$ ....

$\frac{1}{4}$ ....

7. What is the difference in cost between the following two calls?

a. To Boston, Massachusetts, person-to-person, on Tuesday at 12 noon, for 10 minutes. The initial 3-minute charge is $2.85 and each additional minute costs $.29.

Init. 3 min. ....

Add. 7 min. ....

Total cost ....

b. To Boston, Massachusetts, direct-distance dialed, on Sunday at 12 noon, for 10 minutes. The initial 1-minute charge is $.18 and each additional minute costs $.12.

Init. 1 min. ....

Add. 9 min. ....

Total cost ....

The difference in cost is ....

8. Write the weight shown on the scale for each letter. Compute the mailing cost for a first-class rate of $.25 for the first ounce or fraction and $.20 for each additional ounce or fraction.

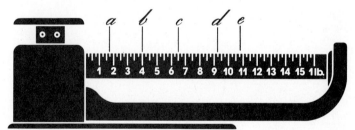

Letter	Weight	Cost
a		
b		
c		
d		
e		

41

SKILLS SURVEY

You have seen how useful math skills are in your daily activities. The exercises in this section will help sharpen your skills.

1. Add.

```
     10              457
      5             3214
 +  204               62
                +    135
```

```
 $29.75          $10.00
   6.82          131.16
    .49             .08
 +  2.63         + 40.05
```

$4.55 + $.89 + $24.50 = ...

2. Subtract.

```
   6879            341
  −2765           −265
```

```
  $8.25          $25.43
  −4.15          − 9.39
```

$128.78 − $32.69 = ...

3. Multiply.

```
   2743           2135
  × 50           ×  32
```

```
    .87          65.23
   ×3           ×  .05
```

4.35 × .25 = ...

4. Divide.

```
 2)848          32)3968
```

```
26)55.90        13)19.50
```

164.30 ÷ 62 = ...

5. Round each answer to the nearest penny.

```
  $5.14           $7.32
  × .03           × .06
```

```
 5)$61.32       32)$73.40
```

$101.60 ÷ 48 = ...

6. 8% of $125.00 = ...

20% of $184.56 = ...

9% of $105.32 = ...

7. $\frac{2}{3}$ of $9.72 = ...

$\frac{3}{4}$ of $8.35 = ...

$\frac{1}{2}$ of $253.64 = ...

$\frac{1}{4}$ of $672.87 = ...

BRANCHING OFF

A. Find out how a taxi meter works. Ask a local taxi driver how much the first fraction of a mile costs and how much each additional fraction is. Figure the total cost of distances you might want to travel.

B. Taxi drivers, waiters, bell hops, and others who offer some kind of service usually receive a tip. Find out how much tip is given in your community. Practice making quick estimates so that you can give the correct tip the next time someone serves you.

UNIT 3

When you plan your expenses, take care of what you really need first. You might even have enough for that vacation or car you've always dreamed about!

Managing Your Money

43

What slip of paper becomes money with a few strokes of the pen? You may write one to pay a bill, or to buy something when you don't have enough cash with you. It's a check, of course! In this lesson, you will learn the basic steps in using a checking account.

 **FACT BOX**

A **checking account** lets you deposit money and take it out by writing a check.

Date MAY 18, 1989	CASH	DOLLARS	CENTS
		5	50
	CHECKS LIST SINGLY	80	25
		15	00
Deposit to Account of *Eleanor S. Angeles*			
	TOTAL ITEMS — TOTAL	100	75

To fill out a **deposit slip**, follow these steps:

1. Write the date.
2. Write your name.
3. Count the cash and write the amount on the CASH line.
4. List the amount of each check on the CHECK lines.
5. Add the cash and the check lines to find the TOTAL deposit.

To write a **check**, follow these steps:

6. Fill in the date.
7. Write the name of the person or company to be paid.
8. Write the amount of the check in numerals with the cents shown as a fraction of 100 ($\frac{58}{100}$).
9. Write the dollar amount in words (fourteen) and the cents again as a fraction of 100.
10. Sign the check.
11. Write what you are paying for.

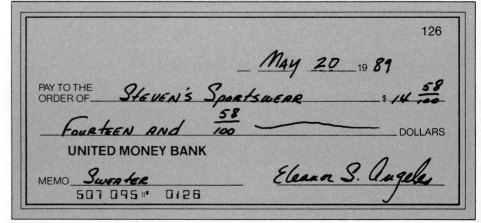

Fill out the deposit slips in Ex. 1-3 using the information given.

2. Your cash deposit includes $10.00, $5.00, $20.00, and 75 cents. The checks are $5.98, $15.00, and $76.83.

	CASH	DOLLARS	CENTS
Date_____	CHECKS LIST SINGLY		
Deposit to Account of _____			
	TOTAL ITEMS **TOTAL**		

Write the checks for the payments in Ex. 4-7.

4. On Sept. 5, you bought a tape recorder from Grand Sound, Inc., for $29.95.

	127
_____ 19___	
PAY TO THE ORDER OF_____ $_____	
_____ DOLLARS	
UNITED MONEY BANK	
MEMO_____	
507 095 ⑪ 0127	

6. You cashed a check for $25.00 on Nov. 10. (Write "Cash" on the line marked "Pay to the order of.")

	129
_____ 19___	
PAY TO THE ORDER OF_____ $_____	
_____ DOLLARS	
UNITED MONEY BANK	
MEMO_____	
507 095 ⑪ 0129	

ON YOUR OWN

Fill out a deposit slip for the cash and checks you may want to put into your checking account. Write a check for a bill you might pay.

	CASH	DOLLARS	CENTS
Date_____	CHECKS LIST SINGLY		
Deposit to Account of _____			
	TOTAL ITEMS **TOTAL**		

1. You have a 10-dollar bill, a 20-dollar bill, and 52 cents. You also want to deposit checks for $40.50 and $14.15.

	CASH	DOLLARS	CENTS
Date_____	CHECKS LIST SINGLY		
Deposit to Account of _____			
	TOTAL ITEMS **TOTAL**		

3. You have three 1-dollar bills, two 5-dollar bills, and 65 cents. You also want to deposit checks for $7.50, $78.25, $10.00, and $21.87.

	CASH	DOLLARS	CENTS
Date_____	CHECKS LIST SINGLY		
Deposit to Account of _____			
	TOTAL ITEMS **TOTAL**		

5. On Oct. 7, you bought a watch from Fine Jewel Co., for $83.97.

	128
_____ 19___	
PAY TO THE ORDER OF_____ $_____	
_____ DOLLARS	
UNITED MONEY BANK	
MEMO_____	
507 095 ⑪ 0128	

7. You need $35.50 in cash. Write a check for this amount on Dec. 1.

	130
_____ 19___	
PAY TO THE ORDER OF_____ $_____	
_____ DOLLARS	
UNITED MONEY BANK	
MEMO_____	
507 095 ⑪ 0130	

_____ 19___	
PAY TO THE ORDER OF_____ $_____	
_____ DOLLARS	
UNITED MONEY BANK	
MEMO_____	
507 095 ⑪ 0126	

BALANCING YOUR CHECKBOOK

 What piece of paper can "bounce"? A check again! If you write a check for more than the amount that you have in your account, your check will "bounce." That means the check is not good and will be returned to you by your bank. You will still have to pay the amount you owe plus an additional amount to the bank as a penalty charge. This lesson will help you keep track of the money in your account by using a check register.

FACT BOX

● This is a **check register**.

CHECK NO.	DATE	CHECK ISSUED TO OR DESCRIPTION OF DEPOSIT	DEPOSITS AMOUNT	AMOUNT OF CHECK	✔ T	BALANCE 100 | 75
1. 126	2. May 20	3. Steven's Sportswear 4. Slacks		5. 14 | 58		6. 86 | 17
	7. May 30	8. Deposit Tax Refund	9. 15 | 25			10. 101 | 42

● Each time you write a check, fill out the check register following these steps:
1. Write the check number.
2. Write the date.
3. Write the name of the person or company you paid.
4. Write what the check is for.
5. Write the amount of the check.
6. Subtract the amount of the check from the old balance to find the new balance.

● Each time you make a deposit, follow these steps:
7. Write the date of the deposit.
8. Write "Deposit" and the description of it where needed.
9. Write the total amount you deposited.
10. Add the deposit to the old balance to find the new balance.

Fill out the following check register for the payments and deposits listed below it.

CHECK NO.	DATE	CHECK ISSUED TO OR DESCRIPTION OF DEPOSIT	DEPOSITS AMOUNT	AMOUNT OF CHECK	✓T	BALANCE
						300 00

151	Feb. 1	Sands Realty Co. (Rent)............$250.00		156	Feb. 19	Dr. T. Lightfoot (Dentist)...............20.00
152	Feb. 5	Bell Telephone.....................15.25		157	Feb. 20	Alex Fashions (Clothes)................38.50
153	Feb. 10	Franklin Electric............................13.43		158	Feb. 21	Pantry Kitchen (Groceries)...........52.18
154	Feb. 14	The Flower Shop (Gift)..................8.50		159	Feb. 22	Texas Oil Co. (Gas credit card).....27.58
	Feb. 15	Deposit (Paycheck)....................198.52		160	Feb. 25	Cash (Spending money)...............25.00
155	Feb. 17	Cash (Lunch money)....................25.00			Feb. 28	Deposit (Paycheck)......................198.52

 Record the deposits and checks you think you might make the first month you are "on your own."

CHECK NO.	DATE	CHECK ISSUED TO OR DESCRIPTION OF DEPOSIT	DEPOSITS AMOUNT	AMOUNT OF CHECK	✓T	BALANCE

SAVINGS

 Saving for a holiday? New clothes perhaps? Regular deposits of money in a savings bank account is one way to save. It's safe and your money earns interest. In this lesson you will learn to use a savings account and to find the simple interest your money can earn.

FACT BOX

In Account with: ELEANOR S. ANGELES				Account Number 10-49104-1	
DATE	WITHDRAWAL	DEPOSIT	INTEREST OR DIVIDEND	BALANCE	TELLER
1 - 1 - 89		100.00		100.00	16B
3 - 31 - 89			1.25	101.25	14A
4 - 1 - 89	10.00			91.25	

A **passbook** is a record of your deposits, withdrawals, and interest earned.

Deposits are added to the balance.

Withdrawals are subtracted from the balance.

Interest is credited or added quarterly: on March 31, June 30, September 30, and December 31.

Interest = Balance × rate × time. The interest rate for the above account is 5% yearly. The interest for March 31 is computed like this:

$$\text{Interest} = (100 \times .05) \times \tfrac{1}{4} \text{ year}$$
$$= 5.00 \times \tfrac{1}{4}$$
$$= \frac{5.00}{4}$$
$$\text{Interest} = \$1.25$$

To take money out of your savings account, fill out a **withdrawal** slip and present it with your passbook to the teller.

1. Write the date.
2. Put your account number.
3. Write the amount in numerals.
4. Write the amount in words.
5. Sign your name.

WITHDRAWAL	THE PASSBOOK MUST BE PRESENTED WITH THIS ORDER

1 April 1 19 89 Account Number 2 10·49104-1

	DOLLARS	00
3	10	CENTS

PAY TO MYSELF OR BEARER

4 *Ten and* $\frac{00}{100}$ _____ DOLLARS

PLEASE WRITE AMOUNT

Signature 5 *Eleanor S. Angeles* _____

INDIVIDUALLY OR IN A REPRESENTATIVE CAPACITY AS THE BOOK READS.

Read the facts carefully and answer the questions in **Ex.** 1-4.

1. Suppose you open an account on January 1 with a deposit of $64. How much money will your money earn at the end of the quarter (March 31) at an interest rate of 5% yearly? ....

What is your new balance on March 31? ....

How much interest will this new balance earn at the end of the next quarter (June 30)? ....

2. You want to withdraw $30.50 from your account on July 1. Fill out this withdrawal slip. Use 10-49104-1 as your account number.

WITHDRAWAL	THE PASSBOOK MUST BE PRESENTED WITH THIS ORDER
	_____ 19____ Account Number _____
	DOLLARS / CENTS
	PAY TO MYSELF OR BEARER
	_____ DOLLARS
	PLEASE WRITE AMOUNT
	Signature _____
	INDIVIDUALLY OR IN A REPRESENTATIVE CAPACITY AS THE BOOK READS.

3. The interest (5% yearly) and balance amounts are missing from this page of a passbook. Fill them in.

DEPOSITORS NAME ON PAGE ONE			Account Number 10-49104-1	
DATE	WITHDRAWAL	DEPOSIT	INTEREST OR DIVIDEND	BALANCE
Jan 1		400.00		....
Mar 31			....	....
Apr 1	65.00			....
Jun 30			....	....
Jul 1		75.75		....
Sep 30			....	....

4. Penny Savings Bank offers higher yearly interest rates on time savings: 6% if the deposit is kept in the bank for 1 year, 7% on 2-year time deposits, and 8% on 3-year accounts. If the deposit is withdrawn before maturity (end of term), the interest is less. How much will the following amounts earn at the end of each term?

Amount of deposit	Interest on		
	1-year account	2-year account	3-year account
$5000			
$7500			
$1350			

DEPOSITORS NAME ON PAGE ONE			Account Number 10-49104-1	
DATE	WITHDRAWAL	DEPOSIT	INTEREST OR DIVIDEND	BALANCE

ON YOUR OWN

Fill in this passbook page with the deposits and withdrawals you might make during a 3-month period.

49

Budgeting

Earning money may be hard; spending it is very easy! That's why it's important to have a budget. When you plan your expenses, take care of what you really need first. You might even have enough for that vacation or car you've always dreamed about! This lesson is all about setting up a budget and managing your money.

What would you do if you were in each person's shoes in Ex. 1-2? Fill out the budget sheet for each. First find the total amount for fixed expenses. Then adjust the flexible expenses so that each person can save money.

FACT BOX

Budgeting tips:

✎ Find out how much you actually take home each month. Net Monthly Income
= 4 × Amount of Weekly Pay Check
or
= 2 × Amount of Biweekly Pay Check

✎ Deduct from your net monthly income all fixed expenses (those which are the same or nearly the same each month) such as rent, utilities (gas and electric), telephone, fuel oil, transportation, etc.

✎ Adjust your flexible expenses (those which may vary more, or are not needed, each month) based on the money you have available after deducting the fixed expenses. Decide what you need and how much to spend for such things as food, health care, clothing, recreation, etc.

✎ Don't forget to include some money for savings and emergencies.

1. Linda earns $175 a week as a proofreader. Her net income per week is $136.50. Here is a list of her expenses last month.

Lunches	$60.00
Movies	16.00
Rent	200.00
Haircut	17.00
Telephone	12.42
Electricity	13.50
Clothes	61.00
Transportation	30.00
Groceries	72.50
Loan Payment	53.08
Cleaners	10.50

Linda wants to save. Help her to decide which expenses to cut down.

Net Monthly Income: $136.50 X 4 = $546.00

Fixed Expenses

Rent	$ 200.00
Loan Payment	53.08
Transportation	30.00
Telephone	12.42
Electricity	13.50

Total Fixed Exp. $ 309.0

Balance $ 237.0

Flexible Expenses

.... $................

....

....

....

....

Total Flexible Exp. $..............

Savings.. $..............

2. Tim's job at the record store pays $152 a week. His actual take-home pay is $115. Here is a list of Tim's expenses last month.

Entertainment	$80.00
Rent	155.00
Telephone	9.50
Gifts	20.00
Food	60.00
Car payment	68.13
Gas & repairs	40.00
Clothing	50.00
Electricity	12.37
Dentist	25.00

Tim wants to go to night school. He needs to save at least $100 a month. Help him work out a budget.

Net Monthly Income: $..................

Fixed Expenses

.... $..................

....

....

....

....

Total Fixed Exp. $..................

Balance $..................

Flexible Expenses

.... $..................

....

....

....

Total Flexible Exp. $..................

Savings $..................

ON YOUR OWN

Now it's your money you must budget. How much do you receive each month? Remember, take care of what you really need first. Then assign what's left to your other expenses. If you want to save for something you really want, you can do it! Work out your budget and stick to it!

Net Monthly Income: $..................

Fixed Expenses

.... $..................

....

....

....

....

Total Fixed Exp. $..................

Balance $..................

Flexible Expenses

.... $..................

....

....

....

....

Total Flexible Exp. $..................

Savings $..................

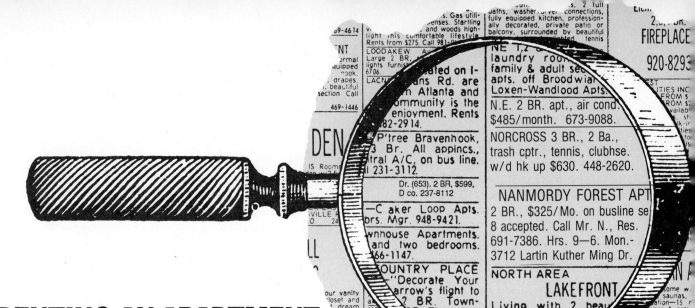

RENTING AN APARTMENT

Is looking for an apartment like decoding a secret message? All the codes in the ads are about rent, fees, and other expenses. If you take some time to learn exactly what the ads say, finding the actual cost of renting a home is not a great mystery!

Which apartment should the persons in Ex. 1-2 rent? Read the facts about them and help them choose. Remember to include transportation costs in making your decision.

1. Rose Chan's net monthly income is $1,800. She wants to rent either apartment A or B. She can walk to work from A, but the utilities will cost her at least $45 a month. She has to ride from B at $1.00 a ride for 40 trips a month.

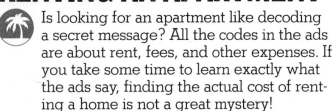

A — Main St. Studio. Lge rm. with kit & bth. $590 plus util. Call eves. 672-4785.

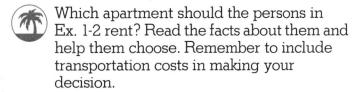

B — UPTOWN EFFCY. Luxury apt with livrm, kit. and full bth. $590 incl util. Call Supt. 699-9424.

Actual Costs	A	B
Rent	$590	$590
Utilities	45	0
Transportation	0	40
TOTAL MONTHLY COST	$635	$630

Can Rose pay the total monthly cost for each apartment? ___Yes___

Which apartment should she rent? ___B___

2. Jimmy Santos' weekly paycheck is $324 or ...... monthly. His budget for rent and transportation is 35% of his monthly income. How much is this? ...... Utilities cost about $25 a month. Jimmy can walk to work from apartment B. The cost of transportation from apartment A is $1.50 a trip, and Jimmy makes at least 40 trips a month.

A	Broad & 16th (southside) 1 BR, Lr, bth, eat-in kit. Incl. util. $400/month 332-0687	
B	Snyder & Hunting Park (north) 1st flr, mod, 3½ rms. $400/month plus util. 485-2327.	

Actual Costs	A	B
Rent	....	....
Utilities	....	....
Transportation	....	....
TOTAL MONTHLY COST	....	....

Can Jimmy pay the total monthly cost for each apartment? ....

Which apartment should Jimmy rent? ....

ON YOUR OWN

You have a choice between these two apartments. Apartment A is within a one-ride zone so that a one-way trip to work will cost only $1.00. Apartment B requires two rides each time you go to work. The average cost of utilities is $19.00.

A	1 BR Apt North Hills Mod, furn, nr park. High flr. Immed occup. $450 plus util.	
B	1 Bdrm Apt South Shore Lge rms, kit with d/w. $390 plus util. Avail Jan. 1	

Actual Costs	A	B
Rent	....	....
Utilities	....	....
Transportation	....	....
TOTAL MONTHLY COST	....	....

Which apartment should you rent? ....

ARE YOU COVERED?

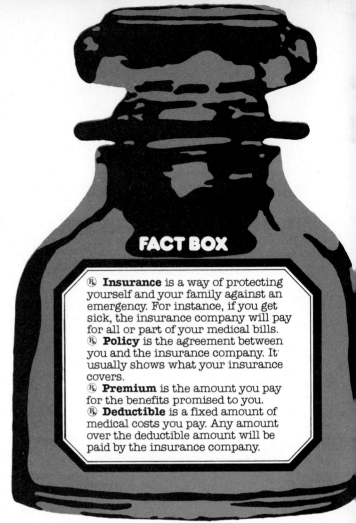

FACT BOX

℞ **Insurance** is a way of protecting yourself and your family against an emergency. For instance, if you get sick, the insurance company will pay for all or part of your medical bills.
℞ **Policy** is the agreement between you and the insurance company. It usually shows what your insurance covers.
℞ **Premium** is the amount you pay for the benefits promised to you.
℞ **Deductible** is a fixed amount of medical costs you pay. Any amount over the deductible amount will be paid by the insurance company.

Being sick can be very expensive. A serious accident or illness could use up your lifetime savings! That's why people buy medical insurance. In this lesson you will discover the cost and benefits of being covered by medical insurance.

In Ex. 1-4, compute the amount you have to pay for each illness if you're covered by any of the insurance plans described in the table.

	Plan A	Plan B	Plan C	Plan D
Monthly Premiums	$13	16	21	25
Maximum Benefits per Illness:				
Room and Board per day	$20	25	35	50
Doctor's Bills (deductible)	$200	100	50	none
X-ray and Lab Fees	$10	25	50	full
Anesthetist	$15	25	40	full
Drugs	$10	20	35	50
Nursing Services	25%	33%	50%	75%

1. CAR CRASH

	Actual Cost	Plan C Insurance Pays	You Pay
Room and Board (4 days at $60)	$240 _(4 x $35)_	$140 _(240-140)_	$100
Doctor's bill	200 _(−50 Deductible)_	150 _(200-150)_	50
Anesthetist	75	40 _(75-40)_	35
X-rays	60	50 _(60-50)_	10
Drugs	30	30	0
Nursing services	100 _(50% of 100)_	50 _(100-50)_	50
TOTAL	$705	$460	$245

54

2. TONSILLECTOMY

	Actual Cost	Plan B Insurance Pays	You Pay
Room and Board (3 days at $50)	$150	....	....
Doctor's bill	175	....	....
Anesthetist	50	....	....
Drugs	25	....	....
TOTAL	....	....	....

3. SKI ACCIDENT

	Actual Cost	Plan D Insurance Pays	You Pay
Room and Board (5 days at $55)	$275	....	....
Doctor's bill	500	....	....
Anesthetist	150	....	....
X-rays	75	....	....
Drugs	50	....	....
TOTAL	....	....	....

4. GENERAL PHYSICAL EXAMINATION

	Actual Cost	Plan A Insurance Pays	You Pay
Room and Board (2 days at $40)	$80	....	....
Doctor's bill	50	....	....
X-rays	25	....	....
TOTAL	....	....	....

ON YOUR OWN

Talk to an insurance agent about a medical plan for you. How much monthly premium can you include in your budget? List the benefits you can expect from your policy.

All About Credit

You just discovered that you do not have enough money to buy something you really need. Should you borrow from a friend? Or should you borrow from a bank? In either case, you are using credit. This lesson is all about credit and how to use it wisely.

When you use credit, you have to pay extra for it. If you buy the items in Ex. 1-3 on credit, how much more will you pay?

1. REFRIGERATOR
$350 cash or $50 down and
$28/month for 12 months

Total amount of payments	$386
Less cash price	350
Cost of credit	$ 36

(margin calculations: $28 ×12, 5 6, 28, $336, +5, $386 ← $38)

2. CASSETTE PLAYER
$5 monthly for 1 year or $52.95 cash

Total amount of payments	....
Less cash price	....
Cost of credit	....

3. PORTABLE TV
12 monthly payments of $21 or $220 cash

Total amount of payments	....
Less cash price	....
Cost of credit	....

How do you find out which loan is cheaper? Find the rate of interest paid for 1 month on each loan in Ex. 4. Use the method shown in this example.

Example: What is the interest rate on a $300 loan for 5 months with an interest charge of $30?

$$\text{Rate} = \frac{\text{Interest}}{\text{Amount of loan} \times \text{time}}$$
$$= \frac{\$30}{\$300 \times 5}$$
$$= \frac{\$30}{\$1500}$$

Rate = .02 or 2% a month

4. Which of these loans has the lowest rate of interest?

....

a. $500 with an interest charge of $50 fully paid after 10 months.

Rate = ...

b. $400 with an interest charge of $40.00 fully paid after 5 months.

Rate = ...

c. $600 with an interest charge of $43.20 paid after 6 months.

Rate = ...

To get a credit card, you must sign a contract called **Retail Installment Credit Agreement.** Read it carefully before you sign.

Use the Credit Agreement Contract in answering Ex. 5-7.

RETAIL INSTALLMENT CREDIT AGREEMENT

I may, within 25 days of the closing date appearing on the periodic statement of my account, pay in full the "new balance" appearing on said statement and thereby avoid a FINANCE CHARGE; or, if I so choose, I may pay my account in monthly installments in accordance with the schedule below. If I avail myself of the latter option, I will incur and pay a FINANCE CHARGE computed at a periodic rate of **1½%** per month (an ANNUAL PERCENTAGE RATE of **18%**) on that portion of the previous balance which does not exceed **$500.00** (subject to a minimum charge of **50¢**) and **1%** per month (an ANNUAL PERCENTAGE RATE of **12%**) on that portion of said balance which exceeds **$500.00**. For convenience, however, there will be no FINANCE CHARGE on balances of $5.00 or less. The FINANCE CHARGE will be computed on the previous balance without deducting any payments or other credits and without adding current purchases.

Notice to the buyer: 1. Do not sign this credit agreement before you read it or if it contains any blank space. **2.** You are entitled to a completely filled in copy of this credit agreement at the time you sign it. **3.** You may at any time pay your total indebtedness hereunder. **4.** Keep this agreement to protect your legal rights.

PAYMENT SCHEDULE	If indebtedness is	$ .01 to 10.00	$10.01 to 60.00	$60.01 to 90.00	$ 90.01 to 120.00	$120.01 to 180.00	$180.01 to 240.00	Over $240.00
	Monthly Payment is	Full Balance	$10.00	$15.00	$20.00	$30.00	$40.00	1/5 of Balance

APPROVED BY: _____ BUYER'S SIGNATURE: _____

---

5. What is the finance charge on a debt of $80.00 for 1 month? ....
(Remember: Interest = Amount borrowed × Rate in decimal form × Time)

6. You borrowed $46.00 worth of goods. You want to pay the full amount next month including interest. How much do you have to pay?
....

7. Your last bill shows a total indebtedness of $150.00. You paid the minimum of $30.00. How much more do you owe?
....

What will be the interest added next month? ....

FACT BOX

● **Finance charge** or **interest** is the amount of money to be paid in addition to the principal or amount borrowed.

● **Down payment** is the cash to be paid at the time something is purchased on credit.

● **Credit card** is a plastic plate which can be used like money.

ON YOUR OWN

If you don't have a credit card yet, you will probably apply for one soon. Go to the customer service department in your favorite department store. Ask for a credit application and fill it out.

FILING YOUR INCOME TAX

 Once you get a job you must file an income tax form every year. It's not as difficult as many tax experts want you to believe! This lesson will show you how to fill out an income tax form using the information on your W-2 form and tax tables.

 Follow these instructions to complete the income tax form on the opposite page for a single individual with no dependents.

A. Print your name and address.

B. Write your social security number. (If you don't have one, use the social security number shown on the W-2 form below.)

C. Find the amount in the box marked Wages, tips, and other compensation on the W-2 form. Write the amount on line 1.

1 Control number	2222	OMB No. 1545-0008		
2 Employer's name, address, and ZIP code Scholastic 1290 Wall Street West Lyndhurst, NJ 07071		**3** Employer's identification number	**4** Employer's state I.D. number	
		5 Statutory employee ☐ Deceased ☐ Pension plan ☐ Legal rep. ☐ 942 emp. ☐ Subtotal ☐ Deferred compensation ☐ Void ☐		
		6 Allocated tips	**7** Advance EIC payment	
8 Employee's social security number 012-34-5678	**9** Federal income tax withheld 1,345.00	**10** Wages, tips, other compensation 13,500.00	**11** Social security tax withheld 1,014.00	
12 Employee's name, address, and ZIP code		**13** Social security wages 13,500.00	**14** Social security tips	
		16	**16a** Fringe benefits incl. in Box 10	
		17 State income tax 675	**18** State wages, tips, etc. 13,500.00	**19** Name of state
		20 Local income tax	**21** Local wages, tips, etc.	**22** Name of locality

Form **W-2 Wage and Tax Statement   1988**

D. You saved $400 at 6% interest rate this year. Find the interest you earned (amount x rate in decimal form) and write amount in line 2.

E. Add lines 1 and 2. This is your adjusted gross income.

F. Write the standard deduction on line 4.

G. Subtract line 4 from line 3 and write the difference on line 5.

H. Write the correct amount on line 6.

I. Subtract line 6 from line 5. Write the amount on line 7.

J. Find the amount in the box marked **Federal income tax** withheld on the W-2 form. Write the amount on line 8.

K. Look at the tax table. In the first column, find the line that matches the amount you wrote on line 7. Go over to the column marked single. Write the amount you see on line 9.

L. Subtract the amounts listed on lines 8 and 9. Read lines 10 and 11 and write the difference on the correct line.

M. Be sure to sign and date the bottom section.

If 1040A, line 19, OR 1040EZ, line 7 is—		And you are—			
At least	But less than	Single (and 1040EZ filers)	Married filing jointly	Married filing separately	Head of a household
		Your tax is—			
8,000					
8,000	8,050	1,204	1,204	1,204	1,204
8,050	8,100	1,211	1,211	1,211	1,211
8,100	8,150	1,219	1,219	1,219	1,219
8,150	8,200	1,226	1,226	1,226	1,226
8,200	8,250	1,234	1,234	1,234	1,234
8,250	8,300	1,241	1,241	1,241	1,241
8,300	8,350	1,249	1,249	1,249	1,249
8,350	8,400	1,256	1,256	1,256	1,256
8,400	8,450	1,264	1,264	1,264	1,264
8,450	8,500	1,271	1,271	1,271	1,271
8,500	8,550	1,279	1,279	1,279	1,279
8,550	8,600	1,286	1,286	1,286	1,286

Department of the Treasury - Internal Revenue Service

Income Tax Return for
Single filers with no dependents (O)

Form 040EZ

1988

A — Name & address

Use the IRS mailing label. If you don't have one, please print.

LABEL HERE

Print your name above (first, initial, last)

Present home address (number, street, and apt. no.). (If you have a P.O. box, see back.)

City, town, or post office, state, and ZIP code

Please print your numbers like this:

0 1 2 3 4 5 6 7 8 9

Your social security number — **B**

Please read the instructions on the back of this form. Also, see page 13 of the booklet for a helpful checklist.

Presidential Election Campaign Fund
Do you want $1 to go to this fund? ▶

Note: *Checking "Yes" will not change your tax or reduce your refund.*

Yes No

Dollars   Cents

Report your income

Attach copy B of Form(s) W-2 here

1 Total wages, salaries, and tips. This should be shown in Box 10 of your W-2 form(s). (Attach your W-2 form(s).)   1 — **C**

2 Taxable interest income of $400 or less. If the total is more than $400, you cannot use Form 1040EZ.   2 — **D**

3 Add line 1 and line 2. This is your **adjusted gross income.**   3 — **E**

4 Can your parents or someone else claim you on their return?
☐ **Yes.** Do worksheet on back; enter amount from line E here.
☐ **No.** Enter 3,000 as your standard deduction.   4 — **F**

Note: You must check Yes or No.

5 Subtract line 4 from line 3. If line 4 is larger than line 3, enter 0.   5 — **G**

6 If you checked the "Yes" box on line 4, enter **0.**
If you checked the "No" box on line 4, enter **1,950.**
This is your **personal exemption.**   6 — **H**

7 Subtract line 6 from line 5. If line 6 is larger than line 5, enter 0. This is your **taxable income.**   7 — **I**

Figure your tax

8 Enter your Federal income tax withheld from Box 9 of your W-2 form(s).   8 — **J**

9 Use the **single** column in the tax table on pages 37–42 of the Form 1040A/1040EZ booklet to find the **tax** on the amount shown on **line 7** above. Enter the amount of tax.   9 — **K**

Refund or amount you owe

Attach tax payment here

10 If line 8 is larger than line 9, subtract line 9 from line 8. Enter the **amount of your refund.**   10 — **L**

11 If line 9 is larger than line 8, subtract line 8 from line 9. Enter the **amount you owe.** Attach check or money order for the full amount, payable to "Internal Revenue Service."   11

Sign your return

I have read this return. Under penalties of perjury, I declare that to the best of my knowledge and belief, the return is true, correct, and complete.

Your signature   Date

M

For IRS Use Only—Please do not write in boxes below.

LOOKING BACK

1. Fill out this deposit slip with $25.00 cash and checks for $48.50 and $28.95.

Date_____	CASH	DOLLARS	CENTS
	CHECKS LIST SINGLY		
Deposit to Account of _____			
	TOTAL ITEMS / TOTAL		

2. Write a check for $15.00 to the Parking Violations Bureau to pay for a parking ticket.

_____ 19 ___

PAY TO THE ORDER OF _____ $ _____

_____ DOLLARS

UNITED MONEY BANK

MEMO _____

507 095 0126

3. Show the deposit and check from Ex. 1-2 in this check register.

CHECK NO.	DATE	CHECK ISSUED TO OR DESCRIPTION OF DEPOSIT	DEPOSITS AMOUNT	AMOUNT OF CHECK	✔T	BALANCE

4. You opened a savings account with a deposit of $200.00. If you keep the money in the account for 90 days how much interest will it earn at a rate of 6% annually?

....

5. You earn $275 a week and your take-home pay is $225. How much do you take home each month?

....

How would you fill out this budget sheet if your usual expenses are:

Rent...$ 275
Clothing... 50
Groceries... 60
Loan payment.................................... 45
Grooming.. 27
Utilities 25
Telephone 12
Movies and lunches......................... 60

Net Monthly Income: .... $ ....

Fixed Expenses:

.... $ ....

....

....

....

Flexible Expenses:

.... $ ....

....

....

....

TOTAL FIXED EXP. $ ....   TOTAL FLEXIBLE EXP. $ ....

BALANCE $ .... Savings... $ ....

6. Your net monthly income is $1,100 a month. Your combined rent and transportation budget is $400. Utilities in your town usually cost $25 a month. Choose between these two apartments. You can walk to work from A. A ride to work from B costs $1.00 and you can make at least 50 trips a month. Which apartment should you rent?

....

A	44th & 7th Studio. Walk to work from this lge rm with kit & bth. $375 plus util.
B	84th & 10th Effcy Lvrm, sleeping area, full kit & bth. $375 incl. util.

7. You have a hospitalization plan that pays a maximum benefit of $208 a day for room and board. You are hospitalized for 5 days at $260 a day. How much is the total hospital bill?

....

How much will the insurance company pay?

....

How much do you pay?

....

8. You can pay for a radio for $39.95 in cash. Instead, you decide to pay $4.60 a month for 10 months. How much more do you have to pay?

....

9. Look at the amounts on lines 8 and 9 on this part of the income tax form. On which line should you write the difference between these two amounts? Line 10 or 11?

....

Write the amount on the correct line.

Figure your tax

7 Subtract line 6 from line 5. If line 6 is larger than line 5, enter 0 on line 7. This is your **taxable income.** **7** | 9,084 . 00

8 Enter your Federal income tax withheld. This should be shown in Box 9 of your W-2 form(s). **8** | 1,434 . 00

9 Use the **single** column in the tax table on pages 32–37 of the Form 1040A instruction booklet to find the **tax** on the amount shown on **line 7** above. Enter the amount of tax. **9** | 1,289 . 00

Refund or amount you owe

Attach tax payment here

10 If line 8 is larger than line 9, subtract line 9 from line 8. Enter the **amount of your refund.** **10**

11 If line 9 is larger than line 8, subtract line 8 from line 9. Enter the **amount you owe.** Attach check or money order for the full amount, payable to "Internal Revenue Service." **11**

Sign your return

I have read this return. Under penalties of perjury, I declare that to the best of my knowledge and belief, the return is true, correct, and complete.

Your signature _____ Date _____

For IRS Use Only—Please do not write in boxes below.

SKILLS SURVEY

You have seen how useful your math skills are in managing your money. The exercises in this sectic will help sharpen your skills.

1. Write these amounts in words as you would for a check.

$6.00 _____ $101.50 _____

$58.34 _____ $1200.00 _____

2. Add the amounts listed in each deposit slip.

Date_____	CASH	DOLLARS 31	CENTS 52
	CHECKS LIST SINGLY	109	50
		342	10
Deposit to Account of _____			
Account Number	TOTAL ITEMS	TOTAL	

Date_____	CASH	DOLLARS 185	CENTS 60
	CHECKS LIST SINGLY	34	75
		1200	40
Deposit to Account of _____			
Account Number	TOTAL ITEMS	TOTAL	

5. What is the rate of interest for each of these loans?

Amount borrowed: $500 for 5 months
Interest: $50
Rate of interest: ....

Amount borrowed: $600 for 6 months
Interest: $36.00
Rate of interest: ....

6. How much interest will you pay a year for ea loan?

Loan: $550 at 12% a year
Amount of interest: ....

Loan: $2250 at 11½% a year
Amount of interest: ....

3. Fill in the balance line after each check.

CHECK NO.	DATE	CHECK ISSUED TO OR DESCRIPTION OF DEPOSIT	DEPOSITS AMOUNT	AMOUNT OF CHECK	✔ T	BALANCE
						1420 75
180	Jan. 1	Allen Realty Rent		250 00		
181	Jan. 15	Bank for Savings Loan		75 50		
182	Jan. 18	Grand Sound TV		398 25		

4. What is the total yearly cost of these monthly payments?

Amount: $225   Amount: $68.13   Amount $170.35

Yearly cost:..............   Yearly cost:..............   Yearly cost:..............

BRANCHING OFF

A. Banks offer several types of savings plans. C a brochure from your neighborhood bank and cide which plan is best for you.

B. There are many kinds of insurance—life, fir and theft, automobile collision, credit, etc. Talk an insurance agent and find out which one mig be good for you. However, don't let the agent t you into buying a policy you don't need!

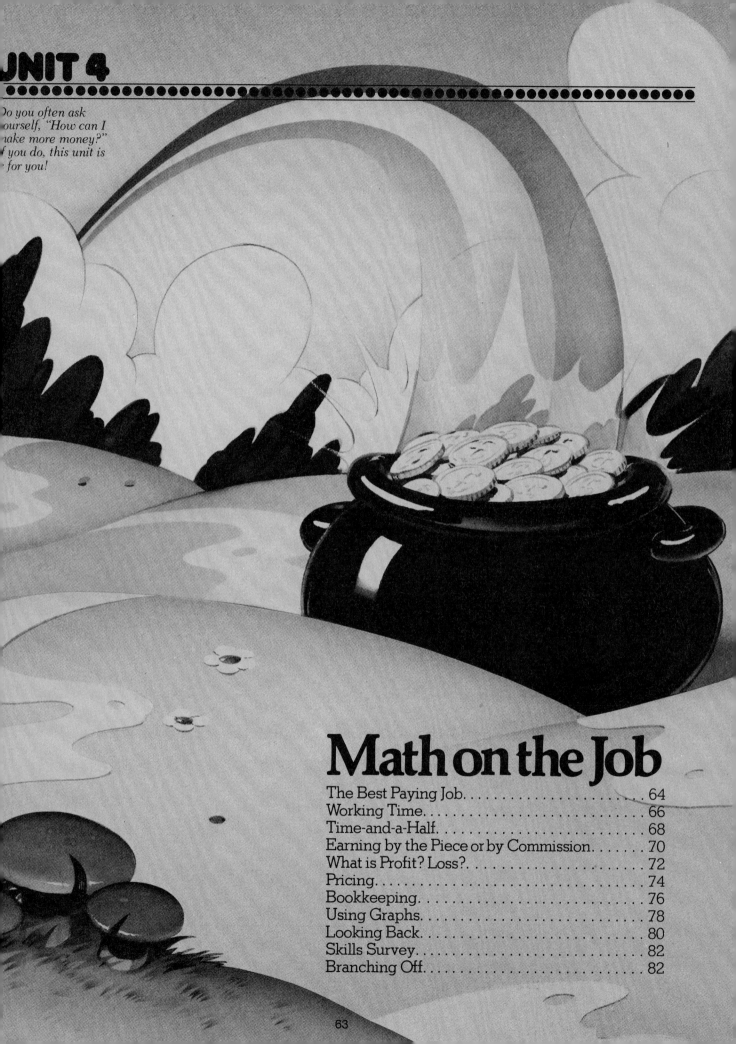

Do you often ask
yourself, "How can I
make more money?"
If you do, this unit is
for you!

Math on the Job

THE BEST PAYING JOB

Do HELP WANTED ads tell you exactly how much you will make when you get a job? This lesson will help you figure the take-home pay you can expect from the jobs described in the ads.

FACT BOX

✔ Hr./Day = total number of hours worked in 1 day

✔ Days/Wk. = total number of days worked in 1 week

✔ FWT = Federal Withholding Tax

✔ FICA = Social Security Tax under the Federal Insurance Contribution Act.

✔ Gross Pay = Hourly Rate × Total Hrs. Worked

✔ Deductions = total taxes and other payments required from employee

✔ Net Pay = Gross Pay − Deductions

✔ Taxes withheld usually come from tables provided by the government to employers. Higher gross pay usually means higher percentage of tax.

PHOTOGRAPHERS
$10.00/hr.
9:30-3:30, 5 days a wk.
Talented people needed for on-location assignments.
Write to: Conte's Photos
1475 Queen St. West
Toronto, Ontario

MODEL $18.50/h
Tues. & Thurs., 9-4 P.M.
Position available for model with department store experience.
X3946 Times

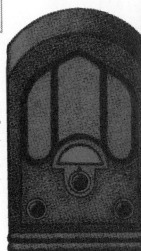

RADIO REPAIR
$6.50/hr
5 days, 9-1 P.M. or 1-5 P.M. Ideal for students and working parents. Will train. Call Benny's Radio, 672-4785.

TRAVEL GUIDE
$8.80/hr.
5 hrs. a day, 5 days a week.
Must speak fluent Japanese.
J-Tours,
201 E. 50, Fifth Floor.

Fill in the missing amounts on the weekly check stub for each job. Follow the steps used in the example.

1. PHOTOGRAPHER

Hr./Day	FWT $46.80
Days/Wk.	FICA $22.50
Total Hrs.	State $16.85
	City $10.92
	Other
Rate $10.40	Total Deductions B $97.07
Gross Pay A $312.00	Net Pay C $214.93
Detach and retain for personal records	

```
A  $ 10.40      B $ 46.80     C $ 312.00
   x      30        22.50       –  97.07
   $312.00          16.85       $ 214.93
                 +  10.92
                  $ 97.07
```

2. MODEL

Hr./Day	FWT $38.85
Days/Wk.	FICA $19.43
Total Hrs.	State $13.99
	City $9.06
	Other
Rate	Total Deductions
Gross Pay	Net Pay
Detach and retain for personal records	

3. RADIO REPAIR TRAINEE

Hr./Day	FWT $19.50
Days/Wk.	FICA $9.75
Total Hrs.	State $7.02
	City $4.55
	Other
Rate $6.50	Total Deductions
Gross Pay	Net Pay
Detach and retain for personal records	

4. TRAVEL GUIDE

Hr./Day	FWT $33.00
Days/Wk.	FICA $16.50
Total Hrs.	State $11.88
	City $7.70
	Other
Rate $8.80	Total Deductions
Gross Pay	Net Pay
Detach and retain for personal records	

ON YOUR OWN

Find the Classified Ad section in your local newspaper. Do you see a job which might fit your interests? Figure out the take-home pay you can expect from the described rates if deductions are usually 25% of gross pay.

WORKING TIME

What time do you come to work? When do you leave? Your answers could mean money! Your salary often depends upon the amount of time you spend working. This lesson is all about measuring your time at work.

FACT BOX

- 🕐 1 day = 24 hours
- 🕐 1 hour (hr.) = 60 minutes
- 🕐 Any amount of time more than 59 minutes should be changed into hours and minutes by dividing the minutes by 60.

```
            1 hr. 25 min.
       60) 85 min.
           60
           25
```

Here are examples of how time is computed:

🕐 Adding time:

```
  1 hr. 25 min.                              3 hr.
+ 2 hr. 55 min.        1 hr. 20 min.      + 1 hr. 20 min.
  3 hr. 80 min.    60) 80                   4 hr. 20 min.
                      60
                      20
```

🕐 Subtracting time:

```
  7 hr. 15 min. =   6 hr.  75 min.
− 5 hr. 45 min.   − 5 hr.  45 min.
                    1 hr.  30 min.
```

🕐 Multiplying time:

```
  5 hr.  45 min.                                25 hr.
       × 5                   3 hr. 45 min.    + 3 hr. 45 min.
 25 hr. 225 min.      60) 225                  28 hr. 45 min.
                         180
                          45
```

🕐 Dividing time:

```
        5 hr.      9 min.
   7) 36 hr.       3 min.
      35
       1 hr. =  60 min.
                63 min.
                63
                00
```

TRY IT!

Add:

```
  5 hr. 45 min.
+ 4 hr. 20 min.
```

Subtract:

```
  8 hr. 25 min.
− 4 hr. 45 min.
```

Multiply:

```
1 hr. 25 min.
     × 6
```

Divide:

```
5) 21 hr. 15 min.
```

The following chart shows the amount of time each employee at Pocket Bookstore worked per day. Find the total time for each employee.

	Sands	Angeles	You
MONDAY	7 hr. 30 min.	8 hr. 40 min.	6 hr. 45 min.
WEDNESDAY	5 hr. 45 min.	6 hr. 15 min.	7 hr. 35 min.
FRIDAY	7 hr. 10 min.	5 hr. 50 min.	8 hr. 20 min.
TOTAL TIME			

Don't forget the lunch and coffee breaks! You don't usually get paid for them. What is the actual time for each of these employees at the Tip-Toe Shoe Shop?

	Finkelstein	Stevens	Hennigan
TOTAL TIME AT WORK	35 hr. 45 min.	29 hr. 30 min.	37 hr. 25 min.
LUNCH AND COFFEE BREAKS	4 hr. 30 min.	3 hr. 45 min.	5 hr. 30 min.

These employees know how much time they worked on their first day. They want to know how much time they might be able to put in each week. Compute the weekly time for each employee.

	Sherman	Cheng	Perez
TIME IN ONE DAY	8 hr. 10 min.	7 hr. 30 min.	6 hr. 45 min.
NUMBER OF DAYS AT WORK	4	5	6
TOTAL TIME FOR ONE WEEK			

Sometimes, you may want to find out what your average time is for each working day. Find the average of each employee at Al's Appliances listed on the chart.

	Kim	Brown	You
TOTAL TIME FOR ONE WEEK	36 hr. 15 min.	38 hr. 30 min.	25 hr. 20 min.
NUMBER OF DAYS AT WORK	5	6	4
AVERAGE TIME PER DAY			

ON YOUR OWN

Now you're a time expert. Use your skills to figure out the average time you spend on each of your daily activities.

TIME

AND-A-HALF

● How does it feel if your paycheck is larger than you expected? Great! Yes, it can happen—if your job pays extra for overtime. This lesson will help you understand overtime pay and how it adds up to your regular salary.

● Figure the gross earnings of the following employees based on their time cards. Follow the steps shown in the example.

EXAMPLE

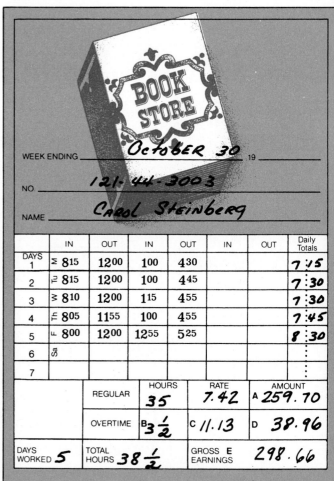

DAYS		IN	OUT	IN	OUT	IN	OUT	Daily Totals
1	M	8 15	12 00	1 00	4 30			7 :15
2	Tu	8 15	12 00	1 00	4 45			7 :30
3	W	8 10	12 00	1 15	4 55			7 :30
4	Th	8 05	11 55	1 00	4 55			7 :45
5	F	8 00	12 00	12 55	5 25			8 :30
6	Sa							
7								

WEEK ENDING __October 30__ 19 __

NO. __121-44-3003__

NAME __Carol Steinberg__

	HOURS	RATE	AMOUNT
REGULAR	35	7.42	A 259.70
OVERTIME	B 3½	C 11.13	D 38.96

DAYS WORKED **5** TOTAL HOURS **38½** GROSS EARNINGS **E 298.66**

A. Regular Pay = $7.42 × 35 = $259.70

B. Overtime = 38½ - 35 = 3½ or 3.5 hr.

C. Time-and-a-half Rate = $7.42 × 1.5 = $11.13

D. Overtime Pay = 3.5 × $11.13 = $38.955 or $38.

E. Gross Earnings = $259.70 + $38.96 = $298.66

FACT BOX

🪙 Many companies consider any time beyond 35 hours in one week as time-and-a-half.

🪙 Overtime = Total Hours Worked − Regular Hours (usually 35)

🪙 Time-and-a-half = 1½ hr. or 1.5 hr.

🪙 Time-and-a-half Rate = Hourly Rate × 1.5

🪙 Overtime Pay = Overtime × Time-and-a-half Rate

🪙 Regular Pay = Hourly Rate × Regular Hours (usually 35)

🪙 Gross Earnings = Regular Pay + Overtime Pay

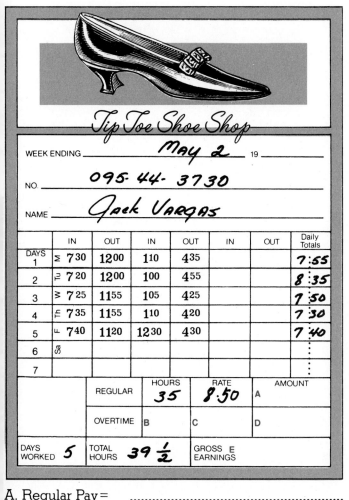

Tip Toe Shoe Shop

WEEK ENDING _____ May 2 _____ 19 ____

NO. ____ 095-44-3730 ____

NAME ____ Jack Vargas ____

DAYS		IN	OUT	IN	OUT	IN	OUT	Daily Totals
1	M	7 30	12 00	1 10	4 35			7:55
2	Tu	7 20	12 00	1 00	4 55			8:35
3	W	7 25	11 55	1 05	4 25			7:50
4	Th	7 35	11 55	1 10	4 20			7:30
5	F	7 40	11 20	12 30	4 30			7:40
6	Sa							
7								

	HOURS	RATE		AMOUNT
REGULAR	35	8.50	A	
OVERTIME	B	C	D	

DAYS WORKED	5	TOTAL HOURS	39 ½	GROSS EARNINGS	E

A. Regular Pay = ...

B. Overtime = ...

C. Time-and-a-half Rate = ...

D. Overtime Pay = ...

E. Gross Earnings = ...

Choose a job that you would like to have. Fill out a time card with the hours that you think you would spend on the job. Include overtime. Choose an hourly rate and then figure out the total hours worked per week, your regular pay, overtime pay, and gross earnings.

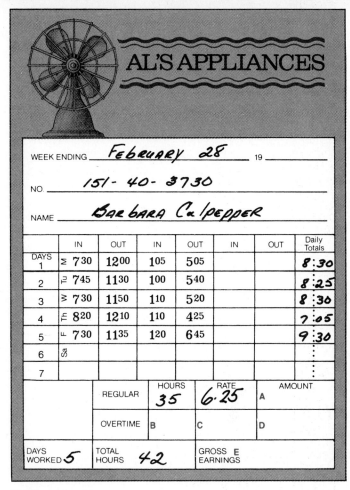

AL'S APPLIANCES

WEEK ENDING ____ February 28 ____ 19 ____

NO. ____ 151-40-3730 ____

NAME ____ Barbara Culpepper ____

DAYS		IN	OUT	IN	OUT	IN	OUT	Daily Totals
1	M	7 30	12 00	1 05	5 05			8:30
2	Tu	7 45	11 30	1 00	5 40			8:25
3	W	7 30	11 50	1 10	5 20			8:30
4	Th	8 20	12 10	1 10	4 25			7:05
5	F	7 30	11 35	1 20	6 45			9:30
6	Sa							
7								

	HOURS	RATE		AMOUNT
REGULAR	35	6.25	A	
OVERTIME	B	C	D	

DAYS WORKED	5	TOTAL HOURS	42	GROSS EARNINGS	E

A. Regular Pay = ...

B. Overtime = ...

C. Time-and-a-half Rate = ...

D. Overtime Pay = ...

E. Gross Earnings = ...

WEEK ENDING _____ 19 ____

NO. _____

NAME _____

DAYS		IN	OUT	IN	OUT	IN	OUT	Daily Totals
1	M							
2	Tu							
3	W							
4	Th							
5	F							
6	Sa							
7								

	HOURS	RATE	AMOUNT
REGULAR			
OVERTIME			

DAYS WORKED		TOTAL HOURS		GROSS EARNINGS	

EARNING BY THE PIECE OR BY COMMISSION

● What rewards do you get for working hard? If your pay is based on the number of things you make or sell, the rewards of hard work are visible: you earn more when you make or sell more! This lesson will help you understand how piecework earnings and commission on sales are computed.

● Read the facts about each person carefully. Then compute his or her earnings.

FACT BOX

● Piecework earnings=Piece rate × Number of pieces made.

● Piece rate=Amount of money earned on each piece sold.

Example: A jewelmaker earns $2.60 for each piece of jewelry. How much will he or she earn for making 56 pieces?

Piecework earnings=$2.60 × 56
=$145.60

● Commission is a percentage of a salesperson's total sales.

Example: Suppose you sell books at 15% commission. How much will you earn if your total sales amount to $7,500?

Commission=15% of $7,500
=.15 × 7500
=$1,125

1.

Susan makes canvas bags at a piece rate of $1.39. When she makes 95 bags in one week, what is her weekly pay? Susan's Earnings =

.... × ....

= ....

2.

Mark makes belts in 3 sizes. The piece rates for each size are: small = $.50, medium = $.75, and large = $1.00. Compute Mark's total earnings on the chart.

Size	Number of Belts Made	Piece Rate	Earnings
Small	25		
Medium	29		
Large	27		
TOTAL			

3.

Elena Carlos sold a house for $145,000. If her commission is 5%, how much did she earn?

Commission=

.... % of $ ....

= .... × ....

= $ ....

4.

Suppose you earn $.39 for each record that you sell for $6.50. What percent commission are you being paid?

Percent commission = $\dfrac{\text{Earnings}}{\text{Sales}} \times 100$

$$= \dfrac{\$.39}{\$6.50} \times 100 \qquad 6\,50\overline{)\begin{array}{r} .06 \\ 39.00 \\ \underline{39\,00} \end{array}}$$

= .... × ....

= .... %

5. Max Parker, a travel agent, earns different commissions for different types of travel. Compute his earnings on the sales listed on this chart.

Type of Travel	% Commission	Amount of Sale Excluding Tax	Earnings
Regular Trips	7%	$455	
Charters	5%	$699	
Escorted Tours	10%	$550	
Transportation & Hotel Packages	11%	$861	

6. Compute the percent commission for the following:

Earnings	Amount of Sale	Percent Commission
$.12	$.50	....
$450	$9,000	....
$1.80	$15	....

ON YOUR OWN

You have seen many different ways of earning. Choose 3 different jobs described in previous pages. Then compute the earnings for each job. Which one would you rather have?

What Is Profit? Loss?

SKATES FOR SALE

● When you buy a pair of skates for $10.00 and sell them for $15.00, your profit is $5.00. But suppose you spend $7.00 for ads before you sell the skates? Then you have a loss of $2.00! This lesson will help you understand profit and loss in business.

● Read the following facts and answer the questions.

1. The skateboard that you bought for $12.00 was sold for $14.50.
What was your gross profit? ....

2. You bought a plain T-Shirt for $3.99. The iron-on letters that you put on the shirt cost you $2.50. How much should you sell the T-Shirt for to earn a profit of $4.00?

Cost of Plain T-Shirt ....

Additional Cost of Letters +..................

Cost of T-Shirt for Sale ....

Profit +..................

Selling Price ....

3. When you tried to sell the T-Shirt at your selling price, nobody wanted to buy it! So you sold it for $5.00. Did you have a profit? A loss?

Cost of T-Shirt for Sale ....

Amount Paid to You ....

Difference ....

Is this a profit or a loss? ....

FACT BOX

💲 Total Sales = the sum of the amounts you receive from customers

💲 Cost of Goods Sold = the amount you paid for the things you sell

💲 Gross Profit = Total Sales minus Cost of Goods Sold

💲 Operating Expenses = the sum of amounts paid for doing business (rent, utilities, telephone, office supplies, salaries, advertising, and others)

💲 Net Profit = Gross Profit minus Operating Expenses

💲 Net Loss = the difference between Gross Profit and Operating Expenses, if the expense amount is greater than the profit

💲 Inventory = number of goods for sale × unit cost

CANDLELIGHT SHOPPE

Profit and Loss Statement For the Month of May

TOTAL SALES		$ .... A
COSTS:		
May 1 inventory	.... B	
New purchases	+ C	
Total cost of candles for sale	.... D	
May 31 inventory	− .... E	
COST OF GOODS SOLD		$ .... F
GROSS PROFIT		$ .... G
EXPENSES:		
....	$	
....	.... } H	
....	....	
TOTAL OPERATING EXPENSES		$ I
NET PROFIT (or LOSS)		$ .... J

Prepare a PROFIT & LOSS STATEMENT for this business. Read the facts for each letter carefully.

A. The weekly sales in May were:

First week:	$155.50
Second week:	186.75
Third week:	195.00
Fourth week:	175.25
TOTAL SALES	

B. On May 1, there were 1500 candles in the store and each candle cost $.05.

$1500 \times .05 =$ ....

C. The new candles bought in May cost $200.00.

D. Add B and C.

E. On May 31, there were 2,000 candles in the store at $.05 each.

$2,000 \times .05 =$ ....

F. Subtract E from D.

G. Subtract F from A.

H. To run the store, the owner paid $200 rent, $100 for ads and $95.50 for supplies.

I. Add the amounts in H.

J. Subtract I from G.

Note: If expenses are greater than the gross profit, the difference is a LOSS.

ON YOUR OWN

Suppose you want to earn from making models of spaceships, submarines, or unusual cars. Find out how much the materials will cost. Don't forget to add the cost of your labor! Figure your hourly rate and multiply it by the number of hours you might spend on a model. Your selling price should include your total cost plus some profit.

PRICING

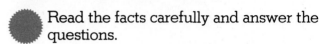

When you buy a stamp collection for $10 and sell it for $11, are you really making money? Perhaps not! The price may not be enough to cover the cost of operating your business. This lesson will help you understand pricing of goods for sale.

FACT BOX

Unit Cost is the amount you pay for one item.

Markup is the amount added to the unit cost to find the **selling price**. Markup is usually a percentage of the unit cost.

The selling price of a skateboard with a unit cost of $9.80 and a 25% markup is computed this way:

Markup = 25% of $9.80
= .25 × $9.80
= $2.45

Selling Price =
Cost of Item
+ Markup
= $9.80
+ $2.45
= $12.25

Read the facts carefully and answer the questions.

1. In order to pay for operating costs and to have some net profit, the Candlelight Shop must sell candles with a 20% markup on cost. What should be the selling price for these candles?

Type of Candle	Cost	20% Markup on Cost	Selling Price
Mushroom	$.85	.20 × .85 = .17	.85 + .17 = $1.02
Peanut	.60		
Animal	.95		
Cartoon Character	1.05		

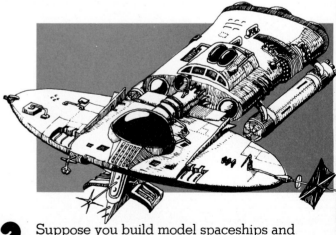

2. Suppose you build model spaceships and sell them for a profit. The materials for one model cost $2.50. To pay for your labor and other expenses, you must price your models with a 400% markup on cost. What is the selling price of one model spaceship?

Markup = $ .... × ....%

= .... × ....

= ....

Selling Price = $ .... + $ ....

= $ ....

3. Find the selling price for each aquarium based on the cost of materials and percentage of markup.

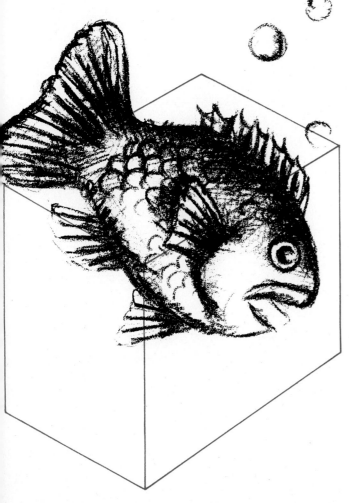

4. Lower prices often invite more sales. If your prices are higher than most stores, you may not be able to sell your goods. The following chart shows how the lower markup affected the total sales of a calculator. Find the missing markups and totals.

Cost	% Markup	Markup	Total Number of Calculators Sold	Total Markup or Gross Profit
12.00	20%	$2.40	200	
12.00	25%		175	
12.00	30%		100	
12.00	35%		50	

Which markup had the highest gross profit?

....

When you have a lot of things to sell, you can easily forget how much each one costs. One way to remember without showing it to buyers is by using a secret code. Here is an example:

NEIGHBORLY
1 2 3 4 5 6 7 8 9 0

The secret code for an item that costs $6.34 is B.IG. What code will be used for each of these costs? $7.76, $9.24, $.53, $67.83.

Size Aquarium	Cost of Materials	% Markup	Markup	Selling Price
Small	$13.50	250%		
Medium	$14.25	300%		
Large	$15.70	290%		
Extra Large	$17.00	310%		

Bookkeeping

● How's business? Your answer depends on what your records show. This lesson is all about keeping up-to-date records of your business activities.

● This is a CASH RECORD. Fill in each missing balance by adding amounts received and subtracting amounts paid out.

Cash Record

DATE		EXPLANATION	RECEIVED		PAID OUT		BALANCE	
June	1	Balance brought forward	545	60			545	60
June	5	New Sweaters			210	00		
June	5	Sales	501	95				
June	12	Sales	750	00				
June	14	Paper supplies			22	80		
June	15	Express Realty			250	00		
June	19	Sales	620	50				

● This is a SALES REPORT. You use it to find total sales. It also shows you which items sell the most and the least. Fill in the missing totals per week in the right column and the totals per item along the bottom.

Sales Report

WEEK ENDING	DEPARTMENTS			TOTAL
	SWEATERS	VESTS	MIXED TOPS	
June 5	200.95	61.50	40.50	
June 12	325.25	170.50	54.25	
June 19	237.80	180.30	202.40	
June 26	420.00	215.60	208.70	
TOTAL				

This is a RECORD OF PURCHASES. It shows the date, payee (person or company paid), and the amount paid for purchased goods. This record is helpful when you want to know the cost of inventory. Fill in the missing totals along the bottom.

Record of Purchases

DATE		PAYEE	AMOUNT PAID		SWEATERS		VESTS		MIXED TOPS	
e	1	Sweaters, Inc.	210	00	210	00				
ne	23	Tops, Co.	195	20					195	20
e	25	Best of Vests, Inc.	88	95			88	95		
e	28	Mixed Tops, Inc.	54	25					54	25
ne	29	Vests, Inc.	90	00			90	00		
e	30	Sweaters, Unlimited	77	50	77	50				
		TOTAL								

This is a REPORT OF OPERATING EXPENSES. It is a detailed picture of how much it costs you to run your business. The report includes the date, payee, amount paid, and what you paid for. Fill in the missing entries and totals.

DATE		PAYEE	AMOUNT PAID		ADS		PHONE UTILITIES RENT		SUPPLIES		OTHER
ne	15	Express Realty	250	00			250	00			
ne	20	Paper Bag Co.	55	40					55	40	
ne	22	Times	60	00	60	00					
ne	25	Bell Telephone	15	40							
e	27	Bus Co.	25	50							
e	29	Advertisers Limited	50	00							
		TOTAL									

ON YOUR OWN

Use the records you have made to find out if Knit Fits is making or losing money.

USING A GRAPH

How can you chart the ups and downs of your business? Use graphs. They're easy and interesting to look at. This lesson will help you understand how to use graphs.

FACT BOX

A graph is a kind of picture. Here are different kinds of graphs. Each one answers a different question about operating expenses.

A. LINE GRAPH

Are your expenses going up, down, or can't you tell? In a line graph, a dot is placed where the vertical line meets the horizontal line. In February, the expenses were $700.

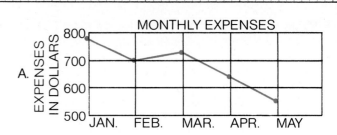

B. BAR GRAPH

Which month was the most expensive or the least expensive? How does one month compare with the others?

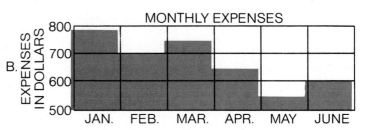

C. CIRCLE GRAPH

What portion of the budget do you spend for each item?

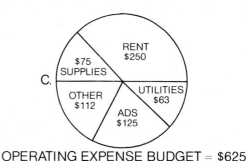

OPERATING EXPENSE BUDGET = $625

Complete this line graph to show monthly sales through May. Place dots on the graph showing these points:

1. Jan.—$50

2. Feb.—$100

3. Mar.—$200

4. Apr.—$175

5. May—$300

Connect all the dots.

Are sales going up or down? ....

Why do you think this trend is happening?

....

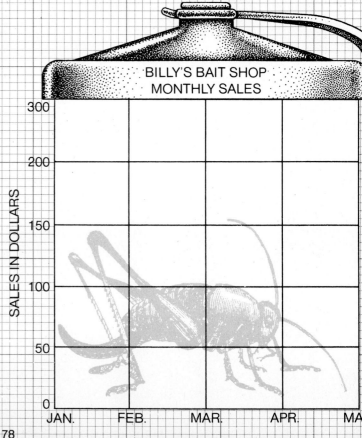

BILLY'S BAIT SHOP
MONTHLY SALES

Make a bar graph comparing the total sales of each item. Here's how: Find the line that shows the total sales of the item. Shade the boxes under the line.

X (sweaters) — $500

Y (vests)   — $600

Z (pants)   — $400

O (other)   — $100

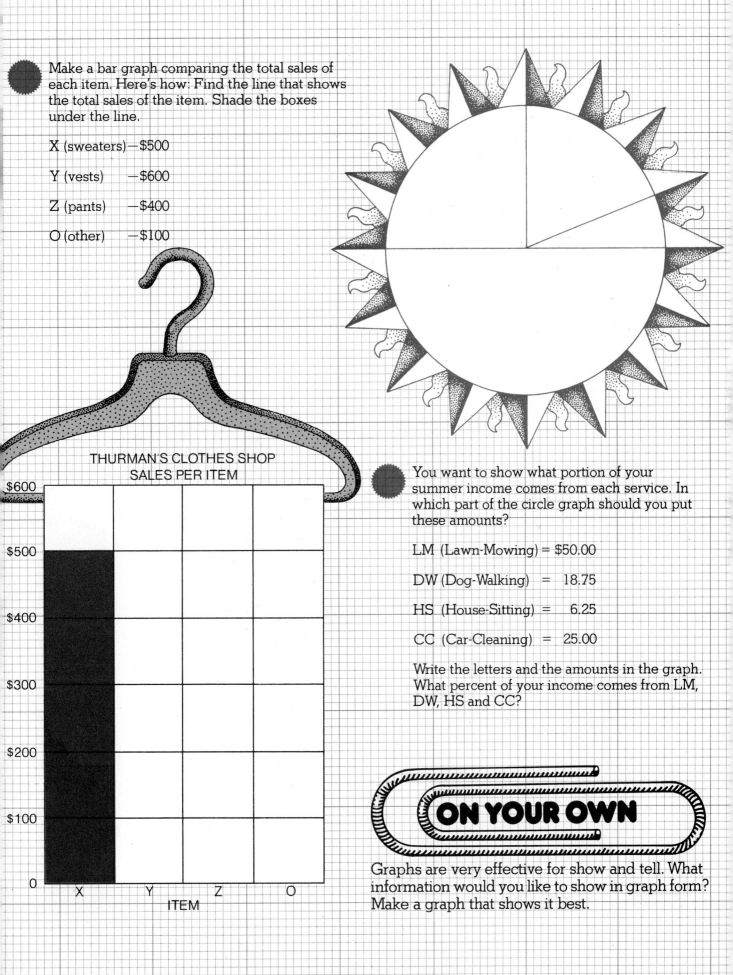

THURMAN'S CLOTHES SHOP
SALES PER ITEM

$600

$500

$400

$300

$200

$100

0

X   Y   Z   O

ITEM

You want to show what portion of your summer income comes from each service. In which part of the circle graph should you put these amounts?

LM (Lawn-Mowing) = $50.00

DW (Dog-Walking) = 18.75

HS (House-Sitting) = 6.25

CC (Car-Cleaning) = 25.00

Write the letters and the amounts in the graph. What percent of your income comes from LM, DW, HS and CC?

ON YOUR OWN

Graphs are very effective for show and tell. What information would you like to show in graph form? Make a graph that shows it best.

LOOKING BACK

1. Compute the total hours, gross pay, total deductions, and net pay on this check stub.

Hr./Day	FWT
7	144.27
Days/Wk.	FICA
7	33.67
Total Hrs.	State 45.28
	City 2.42
Rate	Other .60
$15.90	Total Deductions
Gross Pay	Net Pay

Detach and retain for personal records

2. Stella works 2 days each week. First compute her total hours in the office for one week. Next, subtract the coffee breaks and lunch breaks. Find the total hours she might work in 4 weeks. Then compute her average.

Tuesday	5 hr. 45 min.
Thursday	+ 8 hr. 30 min.
1 Wk. Total	hr. min.
Breaks	− 1 hr. 45 min.
Actual time	hr. min.
Total in 4 weeks	× 4 weeks
	hr. min.

$$\text{Average time per day} = \frac{\text{Total in 4 wks.}}{\substack{\text{Number of days} \\ \text{worked in 4 wks.}}}$$

What is Stella's average? hr. min. ....

3. Here is part of a time card.

		HOURS	RATE	AMOUNT
	REGULAR	**35**	**$6.00**	
	OVERTIME			
DAYS WORKED **6**	TOTAL HOURS	**42**	GROSS EARNINGS	

Fill it in with the following:

A. Overtime hours

B. Time-and-a-half rate

C. Regular pay

D. Overtime pay

E. Gross Earnings

4. Jim earns $.05 for each newspaper he delivers. How much does he make after delivering 50 newspapers?

....

Barbara earns 6% commission for each TV. If a TV costs $399, how much commission does she earn?

....

5. Suppose you bought a radio for $15 and sold it for $25. What was your gross profit?

....

In selling the radio, you spent $4 for ads and transportation. What was your net profit?

....

In order to pay for operating cost and to have some net profit, a photographer must take pictures with a 85% markup on cost. What should be the selling price of each size picture?

Size	Cost	85% Markup on Cost	Selling Price
$2\frac{1}{2}$ by $2\frac{1}{2}$	$.60		
5 by 7	1.20		
8 by 10	2.40		

Fill out this cash record with the following information:

May 1: the balance brought forward is $500.00

May 2: paid $250 rent

May 4: received $150 from sales

May 6: paid Times $65 for ads

Date	Explanation	Received	Paid Out	Balance

Match each graph with the question it answers. Draw a line from the question to the graph.

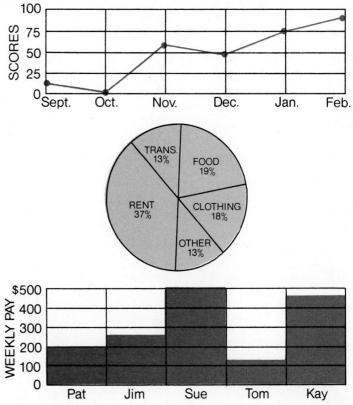

How do you divide
your budget?

Who earned the most or
the least money?

Are you improving your
math skills?

SKILLS SURVEY

1. Add:

```
 13.50
  6.18
  3.10
  1.25           1 hr. 15 min.        7 hr. 20 min.
+  .60          +3 hr. 10 min.       +1 hr. 55 min.
```

27.90 + 11.69 + 6.60 + 2.90 + .90 = ...

2. Subtract:

```
$1575.40        $1113.00        3 hr. 50 min.       2 hr. 10 min.
-  342.20       -  435.67      -1 hr. 45 min.      -1 hr. 25 min.
```

$198.50 − $52.92 = ...

3. Multiply:

$3.50 \times .25 =$ ....

```
$15.50                                          3 hr. 10 min.        4 hr. 35 min.
  × 35                                                  × 3                  × 4
```

$4.20 \times 1\frac{1}{2} =$ ....

4. Divide:

$\frac{1}{5} =$ ....

$70)\overline{145.60}$ $\frac{3}{4} =$ .... $3)\overline{9 \text{ hr. } 6 \text{ min.}}$ $2)\overline{3 \text{ hr. } 12 \text{ min.}}$ $10.60 \div 530 =$ ....

5. Round to two decimal places:

.278 ....   .642 ....   35.791 ....   684.085 ....

17.998 ....   29.6387 ....   99.0084 ....   .00634 ....

6. Compute these percentages:

500% of $3.00 = ...   6% of $450.00 = ...   25% of $184.00 = ...

350% of $.36 = ...   8% of $.84 = ...   1.5% of $23.00 = ...

BRANCHING OFF

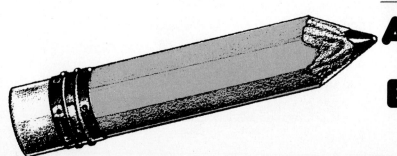

A. Interview one or two people who own a business. Ask them what they like or don't like about being on their own.

B. Find out the difference between wholesale price and retail price. How much discount do stores usually get from wholesalers?

UNIT 5

•••••••••••••••••••••

*rising costs affect
 u, this unit will be
 tremendous help!*

Energy and Money Savers

SAVE A WATT

💲 Do you often wonder why your electric bill is higher than ever? You can't always blame the power company. Sometimes the cause may be you and your appliances. This lesson will help you understand the cost of electricity in your home.

Chart of Estimated Kilowatt Hours Used Each Year by Common Household Appliances.

Appliances	Kwh used each year
FOOD PREPARATION	
Broiler	100
Deep fryer	83
Dishwasher	363
Mixer	13
Oven, Microwave only	190
Range with oven	1175
self-cleaning oven	1205
Toaster	39
FOOD PRESERVATION	
Freezer (15 cu. ft.)	1195
Freezer (frostless 15 cu. ft.)	1761
Refrigerator (12 cu. ft.)	728
Refrigerator (frostless 12 cu. ft.)	1217
LAUNDRY	
Clothes dryer	993
Washing machine (automatic)	103
COMFORT CONDITIONING	
Air conditioner (room)	860
Fan (attic)	291
Fan (circulating)	43
Fan (rollaway)	138
Fan (window)	170
HOME ENTERTAINMENT	
Radio	86
Radio/record player	109
Television, black and white	
tube type	350
solid state	120
Television, color	
tube type	660
solid state	440
HOUSEWARES	
Clock	17
Sewing Machine	11
Vacuum Cleaner	46

FACT BOX

💡 **Kwh** means Kilowatt-hour.

💡 **1 kilowatt-hour** = 1000 watts (1 kilowatt) of electricity used in one hour. For example, a 100-watt light bulb left on for 10 hours used 1 kilowatt hour of electricity.

💡 To figure the yearly cost of electricity used by an appliance, multiply the estimated kwh used each year by the cost of each kwh.

💡 **Cu. ft.** means cubic feet.

💡 **Cu. Ft.** = height × width × depth (in feet).

💲 Use the figures in the chart to estimate the yearly costs of electricity in **Ex. 1-7.**

1.

House of the Adam Family		
Appliances	Kwh used each year	Yearly cost at 9¢ per Kwh
Range with oven		
Toaster		
Refrigerator (12 cubic feet)		
Fan (rollaway)		
Radio		
TV (B&W, solid state)		
Clock		
Sewing Machine		
TOTAL		

2. If the Adams replace their oven with a self-cleaning one, how much more will they pay for electricity each year?

....

3. Suppose the Adams decide to use an automatic washing machine. How much will this add to the total cost of electricity per year?

....

4.

House of the Jackson Family		
Appliances	Kwh used each year	Yearly cost at 9¢ per Kwh
Microwave oven		
Dishwasher		
Refrigerator (frostless, 12 cu. ft.)		
Color TV (solid state)		
Radio/Record Player		
Air conditioner (room)		
Vacuum cleaner		
TOTAL		

5. If the air conditioner is replaced with an attic fan, how much will the Jacksons save in electricity cost per year?

....

6. The Jacksons want to add a freezer (15 cu. ft.), a mixer, and a deep fryer to their appliances. How many more kwh will they use each year?

....

7. What is the total cost of the Jacksons' yearly electricity including the new appliances in **Ex. 4** and **Ex. 6?**

....

ON YOUR OWN

List the appliances in your home. Ask the power company how much 1 kwh costs. Estimate the yearly cost of each appliance based on the chart on the opposite page.

Appliance	Kwh used each year	Yearly cost

City & Highway Mileage

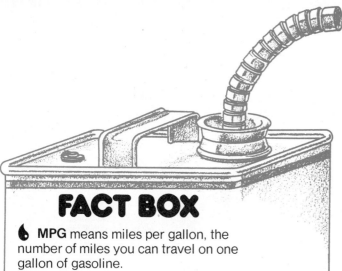

FACT BOX

🛢 **MPG** means miles per gallon, the number of miles you can travel on one gallon of gasoline.

🛢 To compute number of gallons used in the city:
  Divide total city miles driven by the city MPG.
  Round your answer to the second decimal place.

🛢 To compute number of gallons used on the highway:
  Divide total miles driven on highway by the hwy MPG.
  Round your answer to the second decimal place.

🛢 To compute total gallons used by your car:
  Add gallons used in city to gallons used on highway.

 What goes up and what goes down? Gasoline cost and car mileage! Because of rising gasoline costs, car makers are forced to produce cars that use less gasoline for each mile traveled. This lesson will help you understand mileage and how it affects the cost of operating a car.

 The cars listed on the chart were tested on city roads and on highways. Each column shows the number of miles traveled by each car using one gallon of gasoline. Use the chart to answer Ex. 1-3.

CAR MILEAGE CHART		
	City MPG	Hwy MPG
AMC Gremlin	22	34
Buick Electra	15	22
Cadillac Seville	14	20
Chevrolet Camaro	18	27
Datsun B-210	36	48
Fiat 128	20	31
Ford Granada	18	26
Mercury Monarch	16	25
Toyota Corolla	34	46
Volkswagon Rabbit	25	38

1. Three people driving different cars travel 50 city miles and 200 highway miles in a week. How many gallons of gas will each driver use?

a. The AMC Gremlin Driver

City	Highway	Total Gallons Used

b. The Datsun Driver

City	Highway	Total Gallons Used

c. The Seville Driver

City	Highway	Total Gallons Used

2. Suppose the same drivers in Ex. 1 drive 200 city miles and 50 highway miles in a week. How many gallons of gas will each driver use?

	City	Highway	Total Gallons Used
a. Gremlin			
b. Datsun			
c. Seville			

3. Four commuters using different cars drive 120 city miles and 250 highway miles each week. If a gallon of gas costs $.95, what is the weekly cost of gasoline for each car listed below? Use the chart on the opposite page for MPG for each car.

Type of Car Driven	Gas used in City	Gas used on Highway	Total Gas Used a Week	Weekly Cost
Buick Electra				
Ford Granada				
Volkswagon Rabbit				
Fiat 128				

ON YOUR OWN

Choose a car that you would like to buy. Find out how many miles per gallon it can travel in the city and on the highway. Set up your own commuting plan and figure your gasoline cost per week.

gas saving habits

($) VRR-ROOM! So you like fast starts and high speeds! Here's news for you—you're a gas guzzler. Your car may have been advertised with a mileage rate of 30 miles per gallon. Your driving habits can easily pull the mileage down to 15 mpg. This lesson is all about improving your driving habits and computing savings on gas.

($) The bar graph shows you that for the same distance traveled, your car's gasoline consumption increases as you increase speed. Use the graph to answer Ex. 1-4.

1. 8 gallons of gas were used to drive 250 miles at 30 mph (miles per hour). How many gallons were used at 50 mph?

....

How many gallons were used at 80 mph?

....

2. Suppose your car travels 45 miles at 50 mph and uses 2 gallons of gas. How many miles per gallon can it travel at this speed?

....

3. At 80 mph your car will use 3 gallons of gas for the same 45 miles. What is your car's MPG (miles per gallon) at this speed?

....

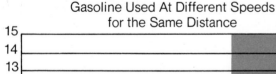

Gasoline Used At Different Speeds
for the Same Distance

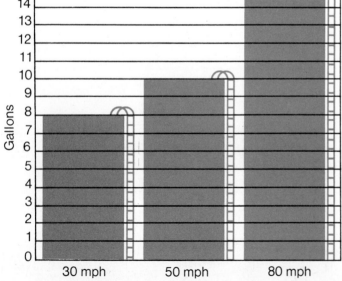

Gallons

30 mph   50 mph   80 mph

Speed

4. Mark's car uses 4 gallons of gas to travel 120 miles at 30 mph. At 50 mph, the car uses 5 gallons of gas and at 80 mph, the amount of gas used increases to 7½ gallons. If gasoline costs $1.15 per gallon what is the total cost of gasoline used at each speed?

Mph	Number of Gallons Used	Total Cost of Gasoline

7. How many more miles can each of the following people drive without additional gasoline if they increase their cars' mileage by 15%?

Driver	Miles Driven Each Year	Additional Miles
Pat Rodriguez	13,500	
Tom Hatch	8,950	
Terry Crawford	18,640	
Donna Santos	21,200	

ON YOUR OWN

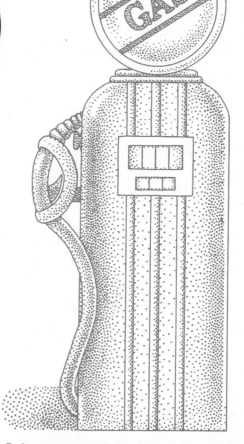

FACT BOX

Gas Saving Habits:

◉ Avoid fast starts and stops. Drive at reduced speeds.

◉ When parked, turn off the engine. A car idling for six minutes uses as much gasoline as driving 1 mile at 30 mph.

◉ Keep your car in good running condition. Have it checked regularly.

◉ By driving sensibly and keeping your car in good shape, you can save at least 15% on gasoline cost.

Use the fact box to answer Ex. 5-7.

5. On a trip to Toronto from New York, Mr. Johnson drove through downtown Buffalo instead of taking the bypass around it. Because of heavy traffic, his car was stopped with motor running for at least 12 minutes. Mr. Johnson wasted as much gasoline as driving .... miles at .... mph.

6. Sandy Lightfoot figured out that by driving sensibly and keeping her car in good shape, she reduced the cost of driving her car by $.025 per mile. How much savings is this if she drives 12,850 miles a year?

....

Ask an automobile salesperson what effects these additional accessories have on gasoline mileage: (a) 8-cylinder rather than a 6-cylinder engine, (b) air-conditioning, (c) automatic transmission, (d) power brakes, power steering, power doors and windows.

DO IT YOURSELF

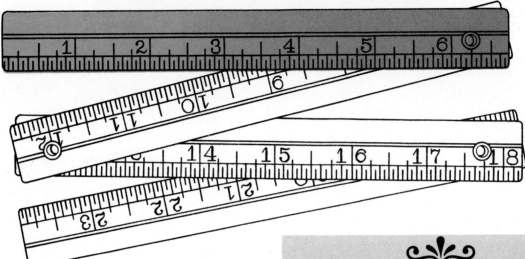

FACT BOX

↖ **Area** = Length × Width (answer will be expressed in square inches, feet, yards, centimeters, or meters).
Area = 9 ft. × 6 ft.
Area = 54 sq. ft.

↖ To change feet to yards: Divide feet by 3.
9 ft. ÷ 3 = 3 yds.

↖ To change yards to feet: Multiply yards by 3.
2 yds. × 3 = 6 ft.

↖ To change inches to feet: Divide inches by 12.
108 in. ÷ 12 = 9 ft.

↖ To change feet (') to inches ("): Multiply feet by 12.
6' × 12 = 72"

↖ To change centimeters to meters: Divide centimeters by 100.
200 cm ÷ 100 = 2 m

↖ To change meters to centimeters: Multiply meters by 100.
4 m × 100 = 400 cm

More and more people are decorating their homes and doing minor repairs themselves. Want to join them? This lesson will help you understand how to measure area in your home so that you can decorate it yourself.

Use the fact box and the ad to solve the problems in Ex. 1-3.

1. Find the area in sq. ft. of each room in this floor plan.

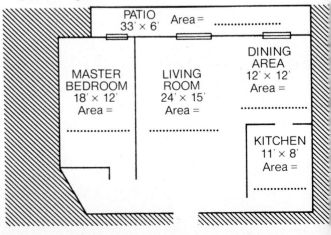

PATIO 33' × 6'   Area = ...

MASTER BEDROOM 18' × 12'   Area = ...

LIVING ROOM 24' × 15'   Area = ...

DINING AREA 12' × 12'   Area = ...

KITCHEN 11' × 8'   Area = ...

2. Fill in this chart with the facts that you need in order to find how much you save if you installed the carpet in each room (in **Ex. 1**) yourself. The patio is done for you.

	Living Room	Bedroom	Dining Room	Patio
Length in Yd.				11 yd.
Width in Yd.				2 yd.
Area in Sq. Yd.				22 sq. yd.
Price per Sq. Yd.	$13.95	$11.95	$10.95	$9.95
Installation Charge per Sq. Yd.	3.99	3.99	3.99	3.99
Total Cost If Installed				$306.68
Total Cost If You Install Yourself				$218.90
Do-It-Yourself Savings				$87.78

← 22 sq. yd. × (9.95 + 3.99)
← 22 sq. yd. × 9.95
← 306.68 − 218.90

3. Suppose you decide to tile the kitchen floor in **Ex. 1** yourself. The tiles that you like come in four sizes. How many tiles will you need in each size? The first one is done for you.

Kitchen Floor Area = ...11.... ft. × ....8.... ft.

= ....132.... in. × ....96.... in.

Kitchen Floor Area = ...12672.... sq. in.

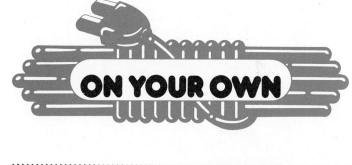

ON YOUR OWN

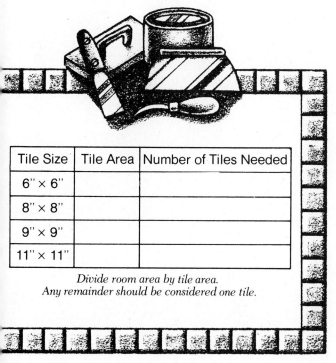

Tile Size	Tile Area	Number of Tiles Needed
6" × 6"		
8" × 8"		
9" × 9"		
11" × 11"		

Divide room area by tile area.
Any remainder should be considered one tile.

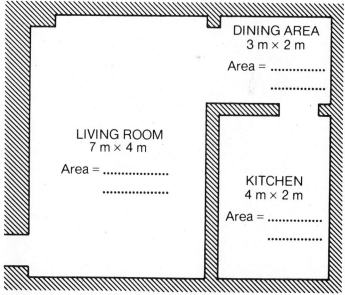

Find the area of the living room, dining area and the kitchen in square centimeters and in square meters.

STOREWIDE SALE!

50% Off on entire summer stock   **20% Off** on items marked with ✻   **15% Off** on all other items

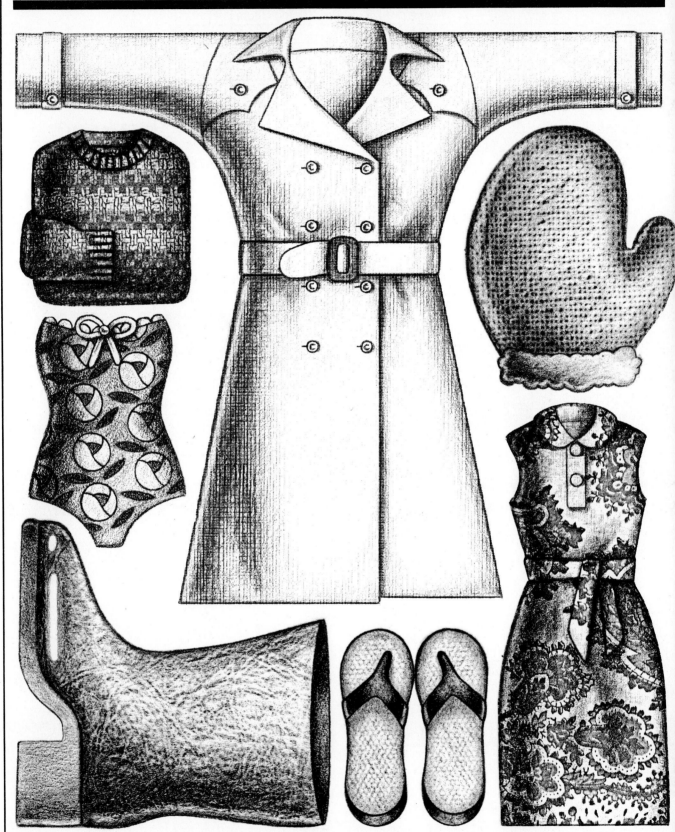

Discounts!

You heard about the storewide sale and came prepared with a shopping list. But, how much will you really save on each item? Can you tell from the ads? This lesson will help you find the amount of discount and the new sale price from given percentages.

Use the ad to determine the percentage of discount for each item listed. Then compute the amount of discount and the discounted price.

FACT BOX

To compute the amount of discount:
✪ Multiply the percentage (in decimal form) by the original selling price.

To compute the new discounted price: ✪ Subtract amount of discount from original selling price.

Item	Price	% of Discount	Amount of discount in dollars and cents	Discounted Price
Swimsuit	23.99			
Sleeveless Dress	27.50			
Bathing Cap	3.65			
Sandals	9.99			
Jacket*	14.25			
Mittens*	7.69			
Raincoat*	18.35			
Boots	25.68			
Sweater	6.89			
Coat	33.30			

Total ....

Total ....

Three people bought the same type of coat in different stores. Find the discounted price of the coat in each store.

Store	Price Tag	% of Discount	Amount of Discount	Sale Price
Honi's	$69.95	20%		
Stella's	$79.60	25%		
Rachel's	$59.80	15%		

In which store was the coat cheapest? ....

ON YOUR OWN

ook for advertised sales in the newspaper. List
e things you would like to buy and figure out the
scounted price from the advertised percentages.

Item	Sale Price
....	....
....	....
....	....
....	....
....	....
....	....

BUY MORE, PAY LESS

💲 How can you pay less when you buy mor
This lesson will help you find out how yo
save money by buying more of an item.

💲 Read the facts in Ex. 1-5 carefully. Decid
if you pay less by buying more.

1. One bar of soap costs 64ᶜ. A three-bar pack costs
$1.90. How much money do you save by buying t
three-bar pack instead of three separate bars?

....

2. A 16 oz. bottle of shampoo costs $3.28. An 8 oz.
bottle costs $1.74. How much money do you save
by buying the larger bottle instead of two small b
tles?

....

A ten-pound bag of rice costs $3.98. You can buy smaller bags in the following amounts:
1-pound bag—49¢
2-pound bag—91¢
5-pound bag—$2.15
How much would ten pounds of rice cost if you buy it in:

a. 1-pound bags? ....

b. 2-pound bags? ....

c. 5-pound bags? ....

How much do you save by buying the ten-pound bag instead of:

d. 1-pound bags? ....

e. 2-pound bags? ....

f. 5-pound bags? ....

A two-liter bottle of juice costs $1.59. One liter costs 78¢. Do you save money by buying the larger container?

....

Read this ad.

a. How much do you save by buying the kit instead of buying the items separately?

....

b. Suppose you don't need charcoal. Will you still buy the kit or buy the items separately?

....

c. You only need an ice bucket, a thermos bottle, and a barbecue pit. Will you buy the whole kit or buy the items separately?

....

ON YOUR OWN

A tour package includes transportation and hotel expenses. Call a travel agent and find out how much you can save by buying a tour package to Europe instead of getting transportation tickets and hotel accommodations separately.

LOOKING BACK

1. Find the yearly cost of using each appliance.

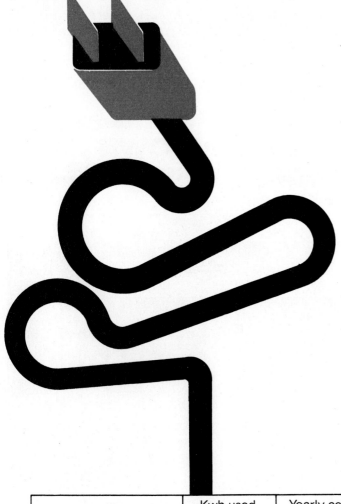

Appliances	Kwh used each year	Yearly cost at 9¢ per Kwh
Self-cleaning Oven	1205	
Frostless Refrigerator	1217	
Color TV	440	
Radio/ Record Player	109	
Air Conditioner	860	
Clock	17	
Vacuum Cleaner	46	

TOTAL COST ....

2. How much would you save if you replaced the air conditioner in Ex. 1 with an attic fan that uses 291 kwh a year?

....

3. Three people driving different cars travel 30 city miles and 40 highway miles a day. How many gallons of gasoline is used a day by eac[h] driver? Round your answer to the nearest ten[th]

	Volare	Granada	Centur[y]
City MPG	17	18	19
Highway MPG	22	26	27
City Gasoline			
Highway Gasoline			
Total			

4. If one gallon of gasoline costs $.95, how much would the Century driver in Ex. 3 spend on gasoline each day?

....

5. Your car uses 2 gallons of gasoline to travel a distance of 48 miles at 50 miles per hour. Ho[w] many miles can it travel per gallon?

....

6. If your car uses 3 gallons of gas to cover the same 48 miles at 80 mph, what is your car's mileage rate (MPG) at this speed?

....

7. Find the area in sq. yd. of each room in this floor plan.

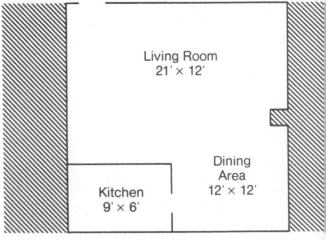

Living Room: Area = ... sq. yd.

Dining Area: Area = ... sq. yd.

Kitchen: Area = ... sq. yd.

8. Three people bought the same type of suit in different stores. Find the discounted price of the suit in each store.

Store	Price Tag	% Discount	Amount of Discount	Sale Price
Jim's	179.50	33%		
Pat's	162.80	25%		
Len's	149.95	20%		

9. Read the ad carefully. Then answer the questions.

a. What is the unit cost of 1 bottle in a case?

....

b. What is the unit cost of 1 bottle in a 6-pack?

....

c. How much do you save by buying a case instead of buying 24 separate bottles?

....

BUY MORE, SAVE MORE

Fruit Juice

1 case	$9.12
24 12 oz. bottles	
6-pack	**2.40**
6 12 oz. bottles	
1 12 oz. bottle	**.46**

SKILLS SURVEY

1. Multiply the kwh by $.09 to find the monthly cost of electricity.

	B&W TV	Radio	Toaster
Kwh used each month	10	8	5
Cost of each kwh	.09	.09	.09
Total cost			

2. Divide the miles driven by the car's MPG to get the total amount of gasoline used.

	Rabbit	Corolla	Camaro	Monarch
Miles driven	1116	1710	1210	1365
MPG	31	38	22	21
Amount of gasoline used				

3. Change to yards.

33 ft. = ...

45 ft. = ...

57 ft. = ...

4. Change to inches.

18 ft. = ...

12 ft. = ...

21 ft. = ...

5. Change to feet.

96 in. = ...

144 in. = ...

276 in. = ...

6. What is the area of the following rooms?

a. Bedroom, 12 ft. × 9 ft. ....

b. Patio, 5 m × 2 m ....

c. Walk-in closet, 48 in. × 56 in. ....

7. Find the percentages. Round your answer to the nearest penny.

25% of $45.37 = ...

33% of $78.50 = ...

20% of $185.00 = ...

8. What is the price of 1 bottle in a package of 6 bottles for $3.78? ....

9. Which is cheaper, 2 for 99¢ or 1 for 50¢? ....

10. A two-liter can of fruit costs $2.79 and a one-liter can costs $1.43. How much money do you save by buying the bigger can? ....

BRANCHING OFF

A. Boxes and refrigerators are measured in terms of volume, usually expressed in cubic feet, cubic inches, cubic centimeters, or cubic meters. Measure your refrigerator at home and find its volume. Make a list of the other things at home that you could measure by volume.

B. You have learned how to measure the area of a square and a rectangle. How do you measure the area of other geometric figures such as triangles and circles?

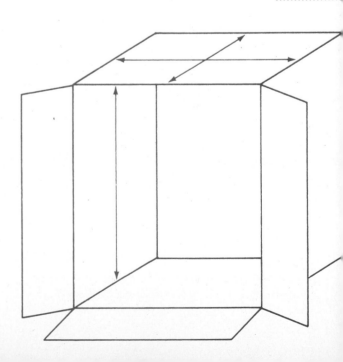

UNIT 6

When you're having a terrific time in sports or travel, you use math skills.

Leisure Math

FACT BOX

W = number of games won

L = number of games lost

Pct. = percent of games won
(expressed as a decimal)

The team with the highest Pct. is considered first in the standings. To compute the Pct. of each team:

1. Add the wins and losses to find the total number of games played.

28 W + 11 L = 39 games

2. Divide the number of games won by the total number of games played. Round your answer to three decimal places.

```
         .7179 = .718
39)28.0000
   27 3
      70
      39
      310
      273
      370
      351
       19
```

Sports news is filled with statistics: records to be broken, number of wins and losses, team standings. You too can compute the statistics related to your favorite sports team. This lesson will help you understand how to determine team standings.

Complete the Pct. column.

BASKETBALL TEAM STANDINGS			
Atlantic	**W**	**L**	**Pct.**
Philadelphia	28	11	.718
Knicks	22	18	.550
Buffalo	16	22	.421
Boston	13	25	.342
Nets	9	32	.220
Central	**W**	**L**	**Pct.**
Washington	24	16	.600
San Antonio	23	18	.561
Cleveland	19	19	.500
Atlanta	19	23	.452
New Orleans	16	24	.400
Houston	15	25	.375

WHERE DOES YOUR TEAM STAND?

Use the Basketball Team Standings to answer the following questions.

1. Which team has the highest percentage of wins?

....

2. Which team should be higher in the standings: Indiana, Detroit, or Los Angeles?

....

3. Which team has a lower percentage of wins: Seattle or Milwaukee?

....

4. Name the team that has the lowest percentage of wins.

....

5. Place the teams in the Pacific Division in order by putting the best percentage record first.

a. ....

b. ....

c. ....

d. ....

e. ....

ON YOUR OWN

Use the Won/Lost columns for these baseball teams to determine team standings. Arrange the teams in order by placing the one with the best percentage record first. (Round each Pct. to three decimal places.)

	W	L
Twins	97	65
A's	94	68
Royals	90	72
Orioles	91	71
Tigers	86	70
Red Sox	95	65
Yankees	97	62

....

....

....

....

....

....

....

BASKETBALL TEAM STANDINGS			
Midwest	**W**	**L**	**Pct.**
Denver	27	13	.675
Chicago	22	19	.537
Milwaukee	23	21	.523
Indiana	17	21	.447
Detroit	17	22	.436
Kansas City	15	27	.357
Pacific	**W**	**L**	**Pct.**
Los Angeles	17	24	.415
Seattle	22	20	.524
Portland	32	6	.842
Golden State	19	21	.475
Phoenix	26	14	.650

SCORING HIGH

When you watch a football game, do you often ask yourself, "How do they get that score?" In this lesson you will learn how to score a football game.

FACT BOX

In every football game the offense is the team that tries to score and the defense is the team that tries to keep the other from scoring. A team can score in the following ways:

⬭ **TD (Touchdown) = 6 points:** carrying the ball into the defending team's end zone by running or passing.

⬭ **FG (Field Goal) = 3 points:** kicking the ball through the other team's goal posts from play.

⬭ **XPt (Extra Point) = 1 point:** kicking the ball through the other team's goal posts after a touchdown.

⬭ **XPtR (Extra Point by Running) = 2 points:** running into the other team's end zone after a touchdown.

⬭ **S (Safety) = 2 points:** forcing the offensive team to move the ball back into its own end zone.

Read the facts about scoring in football. Then compute the scores of the games in **Ex.** 1-3.

1. Game: North Hills High vs. East River High

NORTH HILLS HIGH		EAST RIVER HIGH	
FG =	.... pts	TD =	.... pts
TD =	....	XPtR =	....
XPt =	....	FG =	....
TD =	....	TD =	....
XPtR =	....	FG =	....
FG =	....	TD =	....
FG =	....	XPt =	....
TOTAL =	....	TOTAL =	....

Who won? ....

2. Game: U.S. Senate vs. U.S. House of Representatives

SENATORS

Total TD points = 30.
Number of TDs = ...

Total XPt points = 5.
Number of XPts = ...

Total FG points = 12.
Number of FGs = ...

REPRESENTATIVES

Total TD points = 24.
Number of TDs = ...

Total XPt points = 2.
Number of XPts = ...

Total FG points = 21.
Number of FGs = ...

Who scored more often? ....

3. Game: TV Superstars vs. Movie Superstars

Team	TD	XPt	XPtR	FG	S	TOTAL POINTS
TV	4	3	1	2	1	
Movie	5	2	2	0	0	

Who won? ....

ON YOUR OWN

Every sport has its own system of scoring. Find out how to score a game of tennis, bowling, volleyball, or soccer. Use this score card.

Scores of Your Team or Player	Scores of Opponent

Going Places?

How far are you going? How fast? How much time do you need to get there? These are some of the questions this lesson will help you to answer.

Use the Fact Box and the road map to answer the questions in Ex. 1-5.

1. Suppose you are on your way to Springfield from Greenbelt. You want to take Route 495 in order to avoid Washington, D.C. You can go southeast through Lanham or southwest through Tyson's Corner. Look at the map. Which way is shorter?

FACT BOX

🛣 HOW FAR? Distance (miles or kilometers) = Speed × Time.

🛣 HOW FAST? Speed or Rate (miles per hour or kilometers per hour) = $\dfrac{\text{Distance}}{\text{Time}}$

🛣 HOW MUCH TIME? Time (hours) = $\dfrac{\text{Distance}}{\text{Speed}}$

1 mile = 1.609 kilometers
1 kilometer = .625 mile

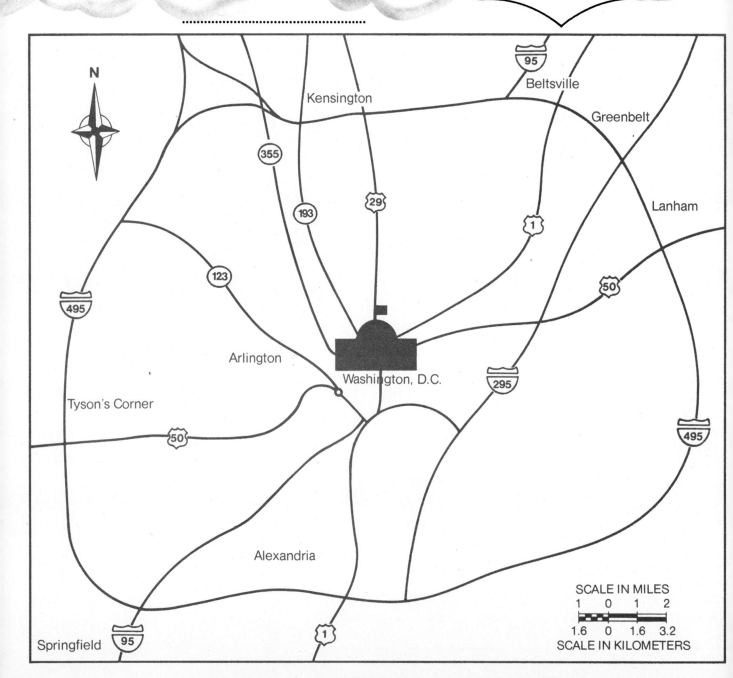

N

95 Beltsville

Greenbelt

Kensington

355

193   29

1

Lanham

123

495

50

Arlington

Washington, D.C.

295

495

Tyson's Corner

50

Alexandria

SCALE IN MILES
1   0   1   2

1.6   0   1.6   3.2
SCALE IN KILOMETERS

Springfield   95

1

2. Coming from Greenbelt on your way to Alexandria, you have a choice between Routes 495 and 295. If you take Route 495, you travel a distance of 27 miles at 55 mph (miles per hour). On Route 295 the distance is 20 miles, but the speed limit is 45 mph. Which route will take less time?

....

3. The Arlington National Cemetery is about 29 km (kilometers) from Springfield. It takes you $\frac{1}{2}$ hour to get there. How fast are you going?

....

4. You circled the Washington, D.C., area along Route 495 at 80 km/h (kilometers per hour) for $1\frac{1}{4}$ hour. About how much distance did you cover?

....

5. From Kensington to downtown Washington, D.C., you have a choice between Route 355 and Route 193. If you take Route 355, you will travel 19 km in 15 minutes or $\frac{1}{4}$ hour. How fast are you going?

....

If you take Route 193, you will travel 10 miles in 30 minutes or $\frac{1}{2}$ hour. How fast are you going?

....

Which route do you think has more traffic problems?

....

ON YOUR OWN

Suppose you're visiting the West. You want to drive from Los Angeles to the cities listed on the chart. Fill in the chart with the missing distance, travel time, or average speed.

From Los Angeles to:	Distance	Travel Time	Average Speed
San Francisco, Calif.	284 mi.	6 hr.	
San Diego, Calif.	195 km		65 km/h
Las Vegas, Nev.		5 hr.	57 mph.

LUGGAGE
How Heavy? How Large?

 Suppose you are making the trip to the Orient that you've always dreamed about. You are checking in your bags at the airport and the clerk tells you, "Your bags are too large. Please pay $142.00 more." Your vacation could end right there! This lesson is all about measuring your luggage to avoid surprises at the airport.

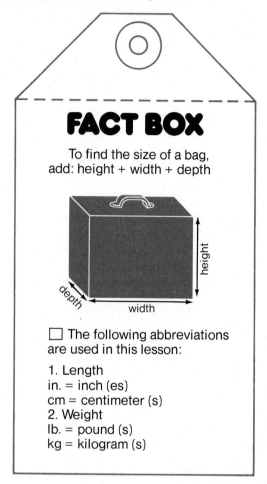

FACT BOX

To find the size of a bag,
add: height + width + depth

☐ The following abbreviations are used in this lesson:

1. Length
in. = inch (es)
cm = centimeter (s)
2. Weight
lb. = pound (s)
kg = kilogram (s)

 When you're going to a foreign country, your luggage is either weighed or counted. Rules differ from airline to airline. This chart shows you the baggage allowances usually given to economy passengers. Read it carefully and then solve the problems in Ex. 1-6.

	BY WEIGHT	FREE BAGGAGE ALLOWED TO ECONOMY PASSENGERS			
		BY PIECE			
		Number of Pieces	Largest Size for Each Checked Piece	Total Size for 2 Checked Pieces	Carry-on Size
Adult or Child (age 2-11)	44 lb. or 20 kg	2 checked-in and 1 carry-on	62 in. or 158 cm	106 in. or 270 cm	45 in. or 115 cm
Infant (under 2 years old)	None	1 checked-in	39 in. or 100 cm	39 in. or 100 cm	Not applicable

1. Compute the size of each bag.

Bag	A	B	C	D
Height	20 in.	61 cm	18 in.	28 cm
Width	26 in.	76 cm	24 in.	41 cm
Depth	7 in.	20 cm	6 in.	14 cm
SIZE				

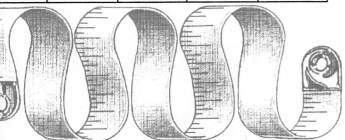

2. Going to Tokyo, you want to bring bags A and C in Ex. 1. If the airline uses the piece method, will you have any problem when you check in at the airport?

....

3. Your carry-on bag measures 13 in. high, 20 in. wide, and 6 in. deep. Is it too large?

....

4. Mrs. Chen has one bag that measures 157 cm. She is going to San Francisco from Hong Kong on an airline that uses the piece method. How large can her second bag be?

....

5. Mrs. Chen's infant son has one bag that measures 33 cm high, 50 cm wide, and 16 cm deep. Will the airline take the bag without extra charge?

....

6. This family is going on a trip around the world on different airlines. If the piece method is used, how many pieces of luggage can the family bring? If the airline weighs the luggage, how heavy can it be in pounds? In kilograms?

Suppose you plan a trip with three friends. You put all your "stuff" together in one trunk. How heavy can the trunk be in pounds? In kilograms?

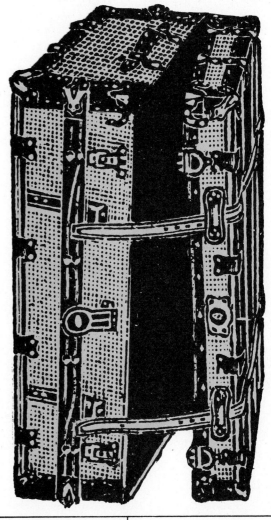

		BY PIECE			BY WEIGHT	
	Age	Checked Pieces	Carry-on	Total Pieces	Total in lbs.	Total in Kg
Father	38					
Mother	37					
Daughter	12					
Son	$2\frac{1}{2}$					
Son	1					
				TOTAL		

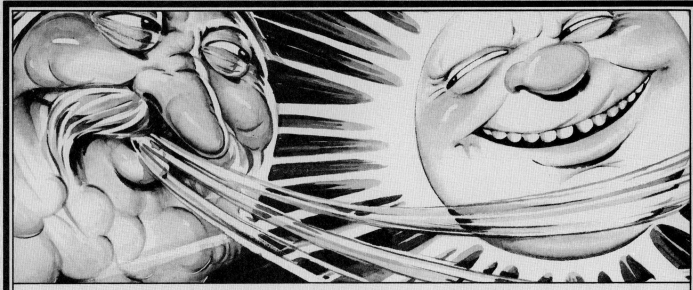

TEMPERATURE CHANGE

FACT BOX

❄ To convert from
Fahrenheit to Celsius:
1. Subtract 32.
2. Multiply by 5.
3. Divide by 9.

❄ To convert from
Celsius to Fahrenheit:
4. Multiply by 9.
5. Divide by 5.
6. Add 32.

Convert 50° Fahrenheit
to ° Celsius.

```
1.   50
    -32
     18
```

```
2.   18
    × 5
     90
```

```
         10
3. 9)90
      9
      0
```

50°F = 10°C

Convert 20° Celsius
to ° Fahrenheit.

```
4.   20
    × 9
    180
```

```
      36
5. 5)180
     15
     30
     30
```

```
6.   36
    +32
     68
```

20°C = 68°F

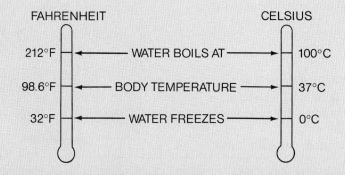

FAHRENHEIT   CELSIUS

212°F ← — WATER BOILS AT — → 100°C

98.6°F ← — BODY TEMPERATURE — → 37°C

32°F ← — WATER FREEZES — → 0°C

 Is it warm or cool? In the United States, temperature is expressed in degrees Fahrenheit (°F). Many other countries give temperature in degrees Celsius (°C). This lesson will show you how to change from one to the other.

 Read the facts in Ex. 1-8 carefully. Then answer the questions. Round your answers to the nearest whole number.

1. Celia Carlos of Toronto, Canada is planning to visit these cities in the United States. She can decide what clothes to bring if the temperatures shown on the chart are expressed in degrees Celsius. Convert the temperatures for Celia.

City	Degrees Fahrenheit	Degrees Celsius
Anchorage	32	
Miami	77	
Phoenix	86	
Seattle	41	
Wichita	59	

2. Scott Jackson of Topeka, Kansas is traveling around the world in April. In every city he visits the temperature is given in degrees Celsius. Convert the temperatures to degrees Fahrenheit for Scott.

City	Degrees Celsius	Degrees Fahrenheit
Athens	15	
Bangkok	35	
Copenhagen	5	
Peking	11	
Rome	18	

3. You set the thermostat in your house at 34°C. Do you feel comfortable? ....

4. Your body temperature is 40°C. Do you have a fever? ....

5. It is 27°C in Montreal and 72°F in New York. Which is warmer?

....

6. The temperature in Chicago is 33°F and in Vancouver it is 3°C. Which is colder?

....

7. If −10°C means ten degrees below 0° Celsius, how would you write five degrees below 0° Fahrenheit? ....

8. What is the Celsius equivalent of 23°F? ....

ON YOUR OWN

List the cities you would like to visit this summer. Find out what the temperature will be from an almanac. Express the temperature in both Fahrenheit and Celsius.

City	Degrees Fahrenheit	Degrees Celsius

Shopping with

FOREIGN MONEY

Canada	1.20 Canadian dollar = 1 U.S. dollar
France	6.00 francs = 1 U.S. dollar
Great Britain	.58 pound = 1 U.S. dollar
Japan	130 yen = 1 U.S. dollar
Philippines	20.75 piso = 1 U.S. dollar
West Germany	1.81 marks = 1 U.S. dollar

A "perfect gift" from West Germany costs only 66 marks! But is it worth the price? This lesson will show you how to convert from one country's money (currency) to another.

1. Upon arrival in each of the countries listed below, you immediately change 500 U.S. dollars to local currency (money). How much do you have in each currency?

Japan: .....**65,000**..... yen

$$\begin{array}{r} 500 \\ \times 130 \\ \hline 65,000 \end{array}$$

France: .... francs

W. Germany: .... marks

Philippines: .... piso

Great Britain: .... pounds

Canada: .... Canadian dollars

The equivalent value of one country's money to another changes from day to day. The conversions given in this lesson may not be valid at the time you actually shop abroad. Use them only to do Ex. 1-7. When you need to know the current value of 1 U.S. dollar in foreign currency, check with your bank.

FACT BOX

$ To change U.S. dollars into foreign currency **X**: Multiply the amount of U.S. dollars by the number of **X** in 1 U.S. dollar.

$ To change foreign currency **X** into U.S. dollars:
1. Divide the total amount of **X** by the number of **X** in 1 U.S. dollar.
2. Round your answer to the nearest cent.

2. You are sending a bottle of perfume to a friend in Japan. It cost you 24 U.S. dollars. How much is it in yen?

....

3. Your friend in West Germany has asked you to buy a tennis racket that costs 35 U.S. dollars. How many marks should your friend send?

....

4. You wish to buy a radio in Japan that sells for 2795 yen. How much is it in U.S. dollars?

$$\$21.50$$

$$\begin{array}{r} 21.50 \\ 130\overline{)2795.00} \\ 260 \\ \hline 195 \\ 130 \\ \hline 650 \\ 650 \\ \hline 00 \\ 00 \\ \hline 00 \end{array}$$

5. A wonderful French dinner costs you 75 francs. How many U.S. dollars are you spending?

....

6. The rain in England forced you to buy an umbrella for 8 pounds. How much is it in U.S. dollars?

....

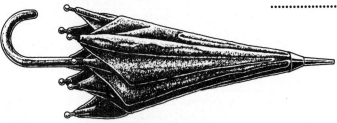

7. A wooden sculpture from the Philippines sells for 250 piso. What is its value in U.S. dollars?

....

8. A car from West Germany costs 25,800 marks. What is its cost in U.S. dollars?

....

ON YOUR OWN

Make up a shopping list for a country you would like to visit. Find out from a bank how much 1 U.S. dollar is in the country's currency.

Item	Cost in Foreign Currency	Cost in U.S. Dollars

LOOKING BACK

1. Fill in the Pct. column to determine the standing of each team. Round your answers to three decimal places.

Team	W	L	Pct.
Astros	76	86	....
Braves	69	92	....
Cardinals	95	67	....
Cubs	76	85	....
Dodgers	73	89	....
Expos	91	71	....
Giants	90	72	....
Mets	92	70	....
Padres	65	97	....
Pirates	80	82	....

2. What is the score for each football team?

Team	TD	XPt	XPtR	FG	S	Score
A	2	2	0	6	0	
B	3	1	2	5	0	
C	2	2	0	3	1	
D	5	4	1	1	0	

3. Fill in the missing distance, travel time, or average speed on this travel record.

Distance	Travel Time	Average Speed
250 mi.		50 mph
	$3\frac{1}{2}$ hr.	88 km/h
640 km	8 hr.	
15 mi.		30 mph
760 km	$9\frac{1}{2}$ hr.	
	$\frac{1}{4}$ hr.	40 mph

Read the facts carefully. Then answer Ex. 4-7.

4. What is the size of a bag that measures 22 in. high, 27 in. wide, and 8 in. deep?

....

5. If the total measurement for two bags allowed by the airline is 270 cm and one of your bags measures 150 cm, how big can your second bag be?

....

6. The total weight of luggage allowed by an airline is 44 lbs. per person. There are nine of you traveling. What is the total weight allowed for your group?

....

7. The combined luggage of a group of seven is 150 kg. Is this within the 20 kg allowed per person?

....

8. Fill in the missing temperatures on this chart. Round your answers to one decimal place.

Degrees Fahrenheit	Degrees Celsius
32	
	37
45	
	21
90	
	19
75	
	40

Use this table to answer Ex. 9-11.

Russia 1.69 rubles = 1 U.S. dollar	
India 14 rupees = 1 U.S. dollar	
Mexico 1,231 pesos = 1 U.S. dollar	
(Remember, these rates change from day to day.)	

9. If you want to change 50 U.S. dollars into the currency of each of these countries, how much will it be in local currency?

Russia: ....

India: ....

Mexico: ....

10. A Russian hat sells for 13.80 rubles. How much is this in U.S. dollars?

....

11. A Mexican serape is priced at 120 pesos. How much is this in U.S. dollars?

....

SKILLS SURVEY

Add the scores in Ex. 1-4. Then find the average of each score by dividing each sum by the number of scores added to get the sum. Round each answer to the nearest whole number.

1.
5
6
4
3
2
6
+4

2.
34
45
36
42
27
+13

3.
125
180
155
200
+160

4.
95
110
124
87
106
100
+ 98

Arrange the numbers in Ex. 5-7 from greatest to least in value.

5.
1.00	....
.02	....
3.20	....
.12	....
4.09	....
4.25	....
3.40	....
1.60	....
.50	....

6.
.600	....
.537	....
.421	....
.708	....
.375	....
.675	....
.500	....
.357	....
.676	....

7.
1.009	....
.958	....
1.010	....
.957	....
1.101	....
.897	....
1.001	....
1.210	....
.960	....

Circle the operation or operations you need to use for each problem in Ex. 8-11.

8. If a TD is 6 points, what is the total score for 6 TDs?

ADD   SUBTRACT   MULTIPLY   DIVIDE

9. What is the total measurement of a bag that is 18 in. high, 22 in. wide, and 7 in. deep?

ADD   SUBTRACT   MULTIPLY   DIVIDE

10. What is your bowling average if you score 120, 130, and 110 in three games?

ADD   SUBTRACT   MULTIPLY   DIVIDE

11. In 29 games the Eagles won 29. How many games did they lose?

ADD   SUBTRACT   MULTIPLY   DIVIDE

Use the following formulas to solve problems 12 and 13: Distance = Speed × Time

$$Time = \frac{Distance}{Speed} \qquad Speed = \frac{Distance}{Time}$$

12. In 5 hours, you were able to drive 250 miles. How fast were you going?

....

13. You drove 100 kilometers at 50 kilometers per hour. How long did it take you?

....

BRANCHING OFF

A. The time of day varies in different parts of the world. If it's 7:00 A.M. in New York, what time is it in Singapore, Paris, London, Madrid, Israel, Hawaii, and San Francisco? Find a time zone map in an almanac.

B. Find out how to score a bowling game. Then complete the scores for each frame below.

| 8 | 1 | | 9 | ╱ | | 5 | ╱ | | ╳ | | 6 | 3 | | 8 | ╱ | | 7 | 2 | | ╳ | | 8 | ╱ | | ╳ | ╳ | 7 | Final Score |

UNIT 7

●●●

This section contains
facts you might need
as you apply your math
skills to real-life
problems.

PLACE VALUES

The value of 5 in each of the places shown on the chart is different. Each place has ten times the value of the next place to the right. A 5 in the hundreds place has a value of 5×100, or 500. A 5 in the hundredths place has a value of $5 \times \frac{1}{100}$, or $\frac{5}{100}$. Another name for $\frac{5}{100}$ is .05.

PLACE VALUES

Billions	Hundred Millions	Ten Millions	Millions	Hundred Thousands	Ten Thousands	Thousands	Hundreds	Tens	Ones		Tenths	Hundredths	Thousandths
5,	5	5	5,	5	5	5,	5	5	5.		5	5	5

Answer the following questions.

1. What is the value of 2 in the hundreds place? ....

2. What is the value of 2 in the hundredths place? ....

3. $\frac{3}{10}$ is another name for 3 in the................. place.

4. An 8 in the thousands place has a value of ....

5. .008 means that the 8 is in the................. place.

Write the following numerals in this Place Value Chart.

PLACE VALUES

Billions	Hundred Millions	Ten Millions	Millions	Hundred Thousands	Ten Thousands	Thousands	Hundreds	Tens	Ones		Tenths	Hundredths	Thousandths
		1	3,	1	3	4,	9	2	0				

Thirteen million, one hundred thirty-four thousand, nine hundred twenty 🖝

Seventy eight and two tenths 🖝

Six hundred fifty-five thousand, two hundred seventeen 🖝

Two hundred thirty-four 🖝

One billion, five hundred six million, one hundred twenty-five thousand 🖝

Eight thousand two hundred twenty-one and five hundredths. 🖝

	0	1	2	3	4	5	6	7	8	9	10
0	0	1	2	3	4	5	6	7	8	9	10
1	1	2	3	4	5	6	7	8	9	10	11
2	2	3	4	5	6	7	8	9	10	11	12
3	3	4	5	6	7	8	9	10	11	12	13
4	4	5	6	7	8	9	10	11	12	13	14
5	5	6	7	8	9	10	11	12	13	14	15
6	6	7	8	9	10	11	12	13	14	15	16
7	7	8	9	10	11	12	13	14	15	16	17
8	8	9	10	11	12	13	14	15	16	17	18
9	9	10	11	12	13	14	15	16	17	18	19
10	10	11	12	13	14	15	16	17	18	19	20

$$\begin{array}{r} 5 \\ +\,7 \\ \hline 12 \end{array} \qquad \begin{array}{r} 17 \\ -\,9 \\ \hline 8 \end{array}$$

The answers to the following problems can be found in the table. Write the letter of the problem next to the answer.

A. $13 - 6 = ?$ B. $8 + 7 = ?$ C. $14 - 9 = ?$

	1	2	3	4	5	6	7	8	9	10
0	0	0	0	0	0	0	0	0	0	0
1	1	2	3	4	5	6	7	8	9	10
2	2	4	6	8	10	12	14	16	18	20
3	3	6	9	12	15	18	21	24	27	30
4	4	8	12	16	20	24	28	32	36	40
5	5	10	15	20	25	30	35	40	45	50
6	6	12	18	24	30	36	42	48	54	60
7	7	14	21	28	35	42	49	56	63	70
8	8	16	24	32	40	48	56	64	72	80
9	9	18	27	36	45	54	63	72	81	90
10	10	20	30	40	50	60	70	80	90	100

$$\begin{array}{r} 8 \\ \times\,7 \\ \hline 56 \end{array} \qquad 9\overline{)54} \;=\; 6$$

The answers to the following problems can be found in the table. Put the letter of the problem next to the answer.

D. $36 \div 9 = ?$ E. $7 \times 9 = ?$ F. $42 \div 6 = ?$

How to use a Pocket Calculator

A pocket calculator can save you a lot of time in solving math problems. Of course, you must tell it what you want it to do. This lesson will help you get more out of your calculator.

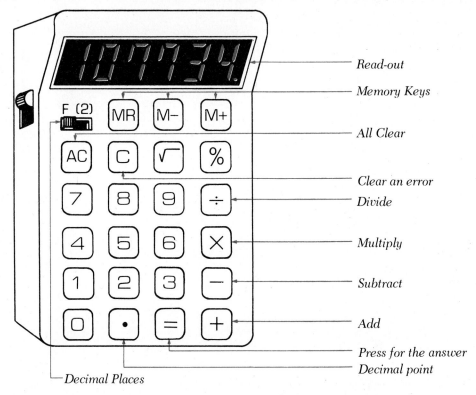

- Read-out
- Memory Keys
- All Clear
- Clear an error
- Divide
- Multiply
- Subtract
- Add
- Press for the answer
- Decimal point
- Decimal Places

Some calculators have different features. The one shown here is a common type of calculator with a memory. The keys must be pressed in the correct order to get the right answer.

Here is an example that shows you how to use your calculator.

To add: 12 + 35

A. Press [AC] to clear the machine.

B. Press [1] and then [2] for 12. Read out shows 12.

C. Press [+]. You want to add.

D. Press [3] and then [5] for 35. Read-out shows 35.

E. Press [=] to get the answer. Read-out shows 47.

Now do this: 27 + 45 − 39

Press the keys in this order:

[AC] [2] [7] [+] [4] [5] [−] [3] [9] [=] Read-out shows 33.

1. To find 35 + 8, which is the correct order for pressing the keys?

[AC] [3] [5] [+] [8] [=]   [AC] [3] [5] [8] [+] [=]

[3] [5] [AC] [+] [8] [=]   [3] [5] [+] [AC] [=] [8]

2. To find 17 + 23 − 8, which is the correct order?

[1] [7] [+] [AC] [2] [3] [8] [−] [=]   [AC] [1] [7] [+] [2] [3] [−] [8] [=]

[1] [+] [7] [2] [3] [−] [AC] [=] [8]   [AC] [1] [7] [2] [3] [+] [−] [8] [=]

3. To find 7 × 8 + 4, which is the correct order?

[AC] [7] [8] [×] [+] [4] [=]   [7] [8] [4] [×] [+] [AC] [=]

[7] [×] [AC] [8] [=] [+] [4]   [AC] [7] [×] [8] [+] [4] [=]

4. Choose the correct operation ([+] , [−] , [×] , or [÷]).

[3] [ ] [5] [=] [8]   [13] [ ] [6] [=] [7]

[4] [ ] [5] [=] [20]   [18] [ ] [3] [=] [6]

5. Fill in the keys you must press to find the answer to each problem.

31 + 23   [AC] [3] [1] [+] [2] [3] [=]

17 − 11   [AC] [ ] [ ] [ ] [ ] [ ]

49 ÷ 7   [ ] [ ] [ ] [ ] [ ]

36 × 12   [ ] [ ] [ ] [ ] [ ] [ ]

3 + 7 + 9 − 8   [ ] [ ] [ ] [ ] [ ] [ ] [ ]

17 − 6 + 11 − 2   [ ] [ ] [ ] [ ] [ ] [ ] [ ] [ ] [ ]

USING THE CALCULATOR'S MEMORY

Often, solving real-life problems takes more than one step. That's when the calculator's memory comes in really handy. This lesson will show you how to use your calculator in real-life problems.

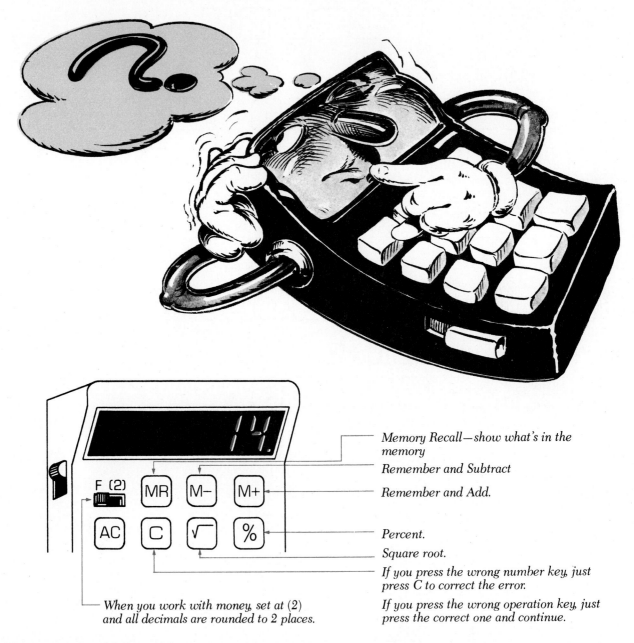

Memory Recall—show what's in the memory

Remember and Subtract

Remember and Add.

Percent.

Square root.

If you press the wrong number key, just press C to correct the error.

If you press the wrong operation key, just press the correct one and continue.

When you work with money, set at (2) and all decimals are rounded to 2 places.

The following examples show you how problems are solved with a calculator.

1. A $58 coat is on sale at 25% off. Find the discount and the discount price. Press these calculator keys in order:

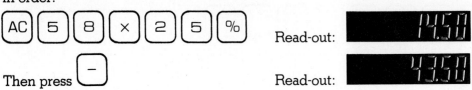

Read-out: 14.50

Then press $-$ Read-out: 43.50

The discount is $14.50. (Some calculators may not show the last zero. The read-out would show 14.5.) The discount price is $43.50.

2. A $35 dress is on sale at 15% off. An $18 sweater is on sale at 10% off. How much would you pay for the two items? Press these calculator keys in order:

[AC] [3] [5] [×] [1] [5] [%] [−] [M+]

[1] [8] [×] [1] [0] [%] [−] [M+]

[MR]

Read-out:
```
29.75
16.20
45.95
```

3. Fill in the missing numbers.

Cost $50 [AC] [5] [0]

off 10% [×] [1] [0]

iscount .... [%]

ale Price .... [−]

Cost $89 [AC] [8] [9]

% Mark-up 15% [×] [1] [5]

Mark-up .... [%]

Selling Price .... [+]

Bill $12.99 [AC] [1] [2] [•] [9] [9]

Sales Tax 8% [×] [8]

Tax .... [%]

Total .... [+]

4. Find the total cost.

hoes $45, 10% off [AC] [4] [5] [×] [1] [0] [%] [−] [M+] $40.50

ocks $1.55, 5% off [1] [•] [5] [5] [×] [5] [%] [−] [M+]   ....

acks $17.99, 15% off [1] [7] [•] [9] [9] [×] [1] [5] [%] [−] [M+]   ....

hirt $10.50, 10% off [1] [0] [•] [5] [0] [×] [1] [0] [%] [−] [M+]   ....

otal [MR]   ....

5. Check the sales slips to see that the totals are correct. The first one is done for you.

....

8.55	[AC]
.39	[8] [•] [5] [5] [M+]
.39	[•] [3] [9] [M+]
.39	[M+]
1.25	[M+]
1.25	[1] [•] [2] [5] [M+]
TL 12.22	[M+]
	[MR]

1.19
2.25
.71
.71
.89
1.09
3.99
TL 10.83

.45
.45
.45
.79
.79
1.08
2.16
1.12
TL 7.29

1.10
1.10
.55
.55
6.52
.15
.15
.15
2.08
TL 12.35

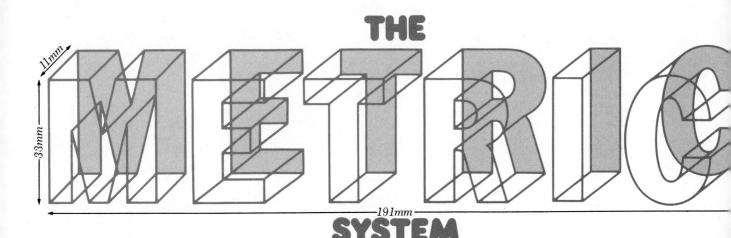

THE METRIC SYSTEM

Meter, liter, and **gram**—these are the basic units of length, capacity, and mass (weight) used in the **metric system,** the measurement language based on ten. It is a **decimal system** using many standard prefixes as shown on the chart below. Each prefix has ten times the value of its neighbor to the right.

Metric Prefixes

Prefix	Kilo-	Hecto-	deka-	(unit)	deci-	centi-	milli-
Symbol	k	h	da	(m, ℓ, or g)	d	c	m
Decimal Meaning	1,000	100	10	1	1	.01	.001

Use the information on the prefix chart to complete this table.

Name of Unit	Symbol	Change to	Operation	Example
millimeter	*mm*	cm	÷ 10	40 mm = ...*4*.......
	cm	mm	× 10	2 cm = ... m
meter	m		× 100	3 m = ... c
meter	m	km	÷ 1000	5000 m = ...
kilometer		m		60 km = ...
kilogram		g	× 1000	5 kg = ...
gram			÷ 1000	2000 g = ...
	mg	g	÷ 1000	4000 mg = ...
	g	mg		3 g = ... m
liter		kℓ	÷ 1000	1200 ℓ = ...
	mℓ	ℓ	÷ 1000	4500 mℓ = ...
kiloliter		ℓ		3 kℓ = ...

THE METRIC UNITS AT A GLANCE

LENGTH

10 millimeters (mm) = 1 centimeter
10 centimeters (cm) = 1 decimeter
100 centimeters = 1 meter (m)
10 decimeters (dm) = 1 meter
1000 meters (m) = 1 kilometer (km)

CAPACITY

1000 milliliters (ml) = 1 liter (l)
1000 liters = 1 kiloliter (kl)
1 cubic centimeter (cm³) = 1 milliliter
1 cubic decimeter (dm³) = 1 liter

MASS (Weight)

1000 milligrams (mg) = 1 gram
1000 grams = 1 kilogram (kg)
1000 kilograms = 1 metric ton (t)
1 metric ton = 1 megagram (mg)

AREA

100 square millimeters = 1 square centimeter
(mm²)   (cm²)
100 square centimeters = 1 square decimeter
(dm²)
100 square decimeters = 1 square meter (m²)

TEMPERATURE

0°C —(zero degree
Celsius) the freezing
point of water
37°C —the normal body
temperature
100°C —the boiling point
of water

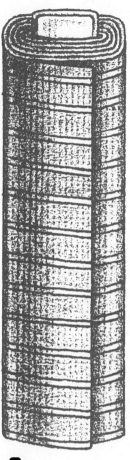

Answer the following questions.

1. Which unit is often used to measure fabric?

....

2. Which unit is used to measure distances between cities?

....

3. Gasoline might be measured with the

....

4. The measurement of a plot of land might be expressed in square

5. A dime is about one

.... thick.

6. To find out how heavy a bag is, which unit would you use?

....

7. A dose of liquid medicine might be expressed in

....

8. The net weight of a box of cereal might be expressed in

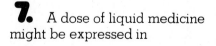

9. Oven heat is expressed in

....

10. The size of a tile is often expressed in

....

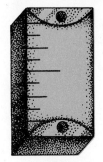

ENGLISH AND METRIC COMPARED

APPROXIMATE EQUIVALENTS

LENGTH

1 mm = .039 in.	1 in. = 25.4 mm
1 cm = .39 in.	1 in. = 2.54 cm
1 m = 1.09 yd.	1 ft. = .3 m
1 m = 3.28 ft.	1 yd. = .91 m
1 km = .62 mi.	1 mi. = 1.6 km

MASS (Weight)

1 g = .035 oz.	1 oz. = 28 g
1 kg = 2.2 lb.	1 lb. = .45 kg

CAPACITY (Liquid Measurement)

1 mℓ = .03 fl. oz.	1 fl. oz. = 29.57 mℓ
1 ℓ = 2.11 pt.	1 pt. = .47ℓ
1 ℓ = 1.06 qt.	1 qt. = .95ℓ

TEMPERATURE

0°Celsius = 32°Fahrenheit   0°Fahrenheit = -17.8°Celsius

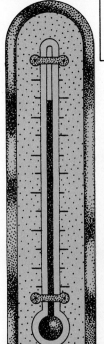

Apply the above comparisons to the following questions.

1. Which is thicker? 3 in. or 5 cm? ....

2. Is a 4 lb.-package heavier than 2 kg? ....

3. Which is the larger container? 2 qt., or 2ℓ ? ....

4. Is 65 km per hour within the 55-mile-per-hour speed limit? ....

5. What is the metric height of a 5-ft.-tall person? ....

6. Which is lighter? 9 oz., or 230 g? ....

7. Which cherries cost less? 10 lb. for $15 or 9 kg for $20? ....

8. Which temperature is warmer? 20° Celsius, or 32° Fahrenheit? ....

9. Is a 62 in.-bag larger or smaller than 145 cm? ....

10. You used to weigh 100 lb. Now you weigh 49 kg. Did you lose or gain weight?

....

These are the meanings of important terms as used in the context of this book.

account—the record of one's money in a bank.

dends—numbers to be added.

ddition—the operation of combining numbers to get a sum.

ea—the number of unit squares in a surface (length multiplied by dth).

ea code—a number that identifies ch telephone service area in a untry.

erage—a number equal to the m divided by the number of dends.

lance—the amount of money remaining in an account after a deposit s been added or a payment has en subtracted.

lance brought forward—the last ance on the previous page itten on the first line of a new page.

nefits (insurance)—the payments services given by an insurance mpany as stated in a policy.

okkeeping—the method of recording the income and expenses a business.

dgeting—putting aside money particular expenses.

lculator—a machine used to mpute math problems.

sh—money that is immediately ailable to spend.

sh record—a statement that ows the balance after adding ounts received or subtracting ounts paid out.

lsius—the Metric System's term ed to express temperature.

ange—the coins or bills you get ck after giving more money than at is due from you.

art—a table, drawing, diagram map that puts together information so that each item can be easily nd.

eck—a written order telling the nk to pay money from your count as instructed.

eck register—a record of deposits

and checks written.

Circle graph—a pie-shaped graph showing how a whole amount of something is divided into various-sized parts.

Commission—a percentage of a salesperson's total sales.

Commuters—regular riders.

Compute—to figure out the answer to a math problem.

Cost of goods sold—the amount paid by the seller for the things he or she sells.

Credit—a loan or borrowed amount to be paid back after the promised period of time.

Currency—money (coins or bills) that is used in exchange for goods or services.

Customer—someone who buys goods or services.

Debit—the amount of money subtracted from an account.

Decimal—a special type of fraction based on tenths.

Deductible (insurance)—initial specified amount to be paid by the insured; anything in excess of that amount will be paid by the insurance company.

Deductions—taxes and contributions subtracted from gross pay to get the net pay.

Denominator—the number of parts into which a whole has been divided; the number at the bottom of a fraction.

Deposit—to put money in a bank account.

Difference—the answer to a subtraction problem.

Digit—the figures 0, 1, 2, 3, 4, 5, 6, 7, 8, and 9 which make up numerals.

Discount—the amount taken off from the usual price.

Distance—the space between two points.

Division—the process of separating a whole amount of something into a

number of parts.

Downpayment—a part of the full price paid at the time of purchase.

Expense—an amount paid out.

Fahrenheit—the English System's term used to tell temperature.

FICA—Federal Insurance Contribution Act or Social Security tax.

Finance charge—interest or amount paid in addition to the amount borrowed.

Fixed expenses—amounts to pay which are the same or nearly the same each month.

Flexible expenses—amounts to pay which may vary more, or are not needed each month.

Fraction—a part of a whole expressed as a number with a numerator and a denominator.

FWT—Federal Withholding Tax, or amount of federal income tax deducted from a paycheck.

Graph—a pictorial representation of related facts or figures.

Gross pay (income)—the total amount earned before any deductions are subtracted.

Gross profit—the total amount of money earned by a business before expenses are deducted.

Income—the amount of money earned from labor or from profit.

Income tax—the tax paid on an individual's (or business') net income.

Insurance—coverage by contract for money losses in the case of fire, death, injury or accidents.

Interest (simple)—a percent paid on an amount of money borrowed or a percent earned on an amount deposited in a savings account.

Installment—one of a series of payments made until the amount borrowed is completely paid for.

Kilo—the Metric System's prefix that means one thousand; often used to mean kilogram.

KWH (kilowatt hour)—one thousand watts of electricity used in one hour.

Line Graph—a pictorial representation of the rises and falls of a line formed by connected dots.

Loan—money lent with interest to a borrower for temporary use.

Long distance—telephone call made between two different area codes.

Mail—letters and packages sent from one place to another at the cost specified by the post office.

Markup—an amount added to the unit cost in order to find the selling price.

Meter—the basic unit of length in the Metric System.

Mileage (MPG)—total miles traveled on one gallon of gasoline.

Multiplication—the process of adding a number to itself a specified number of times.

Net Earning, Income or Pay—the amount the individual takes home after all deductions have been made.

Net Loss—amount of money lost when operating costs exceed profits.

Net Profit—amount of profit after all deductions have been made.

New balance—in a record, the balance which appears after an expense has been recorded and subtracted.

Operating expenses—the amount of money needed to produce goods or services (rent, utilities, supplies, ads, and others).

Overtime—time in excess of a standard work day or schedule.

Passbook—a record of deposits and withdrawals in a savings account.

Paycheck—a written order telling the bank to pay the amount of salary earned by the person named.

PCT—the abbreviation used in team standings for percent of games won in relation to the number of games played.

Percent—one part of a hundred.

Piece rate—amount of money earned for each piece made or sold.

Piecework earnings—income computed by multiplying piece rate times the number of pieces made or sold.

Place value—the value based on the location of a digit in a numeral.

Policy—the written agreement between the insured and the insurance company.

Postage—the fee paid for stamps needed to send a letter or package.

Pound (lb.)—a unit of mass or weight; equal to 16 ounces.

Premium—the amount paid to the insurance company for benefits promised.

Profit—amount of money retained after all expenses have been deducted.

Product—the answer to a multiplication problem.

Quantity (Qty.)—number of items bought or sold.

Quotient—the answer to a division problem.

Ratio—the comparison of two amounts usually named by a fraction.

Record of Purchases—a list of items bought by a business.

Retail—the selling of a product to a consumer in small quantities.

Road Map—a guide to the roads within a specified area.

Route—a fixed course of travel.

Salary—amount earned in exchange for labor.

Sale—selling of goods at discounted prices.

Sales report—a record of the total income of a business over a given period.

Sales tax—additional amount charged on goods and services based on a percentage of the purchase price; it is usually imposed by both state and city.

Savings Account—a bank account in which money is deposited for safekeeping and for earning interest.

Schedule—a chart showing a time table or transportation fares.

Speed—the rate at which a given distance is traveled.

Subtotal—a partial sum; the sum before a sales tax is added.

Subtraction—the process of finding the difference between two numbers.

Sum—the result of adding two numbers.

Table—information arranged in rows and columns for easy reference.

Tax—an amount of money charged by the government on products, services, property, or income.

Team standings—how teams rank based on the ratio of games won to the number of games played.

Temperature—a measure of how hot or cold the climate is.

Time—a period expressed in terms of seconds, minutes, hours, days, months or years.

Time-and-a-half—a rate paid for overtime work usually equal to regular hourly rate times $1\frac{1}{2}$.

Total—the sum or product of a list of amounts.

Unit cost—the actual amount paid by the seller for one item for sale, such amounts are usually marked up for profit.

Utilities—gas, electricity, water, and other essentials in a home.

W-2 form—a statement of income and tax withheld.

Wholesale—the selling of large quantities of goods for resale by another person or business.

Withdraw—to take money out of a bank account.

1 numbers refer to spirit masters.